mad women

THE **OTHER** SIDE OF LIFE ON MADISON AVENUE IN THE '60S AND BEYOND

jane maas

thomas dunne books st. martin's griffin
new york

Author's Note: The names and identifying characteristics of some people have been changed.

THOMAS DUNNE BOOKS.
An imprint of St. Martin's Press.

 Printed in the United States of America. For information, address St. Martin's Press, 175 Fifth Avenue, New York, N.Y. 10010.

www.thomasdunnebooks.com
www.stmartins.com

All photos courtesy of the author except page 74, courtesy of Philip Roth and the Department of Theatre and Dance, Bucknell University.

Design by Anna Gorovoy

The Library of Congress has cataloged the hardcover edition as follows:

Maas, Jane.
Mad women : the other side of life on Madison Avenue in the '60s and beyond / Jane Maas. — 1st ed.
p. cm.
ISBN 978-0-312-64023-1 (hardcover)
ISBN 978-1-4299-4114-3 (e-book)
1. Maas, Jane. 2. Women in the advertising industry—United States—Biography. 3. Advertising executives—United States—Biography. 4. Advertising—United States. I. Title.
HF5810.M33A35 2012
659.1092—dc23
[B]

2011041060

ISBN 978-1-250-02201-1 (trade paperback)

First St. Martin's Griffin Edition: February 2013

10 9 8 7 6 5 4 3 2 1

also by jane maas

Adventures of an Advertising Woman

How to Advertise (with Kenneth Roman)

Christmas in Wales: A Homecoming (with Michael Maas)

"The funniest book I've read since *From Those Wonderful Folks Who Gave You Pearl Harbor.*"

—Jerry Della Femina, chairman and CEO of Della Femina Advertising and author of the bestselling *From Those Wonderful Folks Who Gave You Pearl Harbor*

"Maas's humorous yet authoritative account of her life in advertising during the *Mad Men* era is a welcome look behind the curtain into a traditionally male world."

—*Publishers Weekly*

"A shrewd and witty firsthand sociocultural history of America in the sixties and seventies from a woman's point of view. A smart, funny, irreverent woman."

—Bruce McCall, *New Yorker* writer and cover illustrator

For all those wonderfully sane
mad women in my life

For H[illegible],
My fellow Mad Woman!
I wish you all the best,
Jane

CONTENTS

Foreword by Mary Wells Lawrence xi

1 A Day on Madison Avenue, 1967 1
2 Sex in the Office 27
3 "Get the Money Before They Screw You" 51
4 Women and Children Last 71
5 The Three-Martini Lunch and Other Vices 93
6 A Different Century, a Different World 113
7 Bang Bang, You're Dead (the Creative Revolution Kills) 135
8 Sex in Advertising 157
9 Why I Love New York 173
10 The Queen and I 191
11 Have You Really Come Such a Long Way, Baby? 203
Epilogue: The War Over *Mad Men* 213

Acknowledgments 215
Index 219

Foreword by Mary Wells Lawrence

This book of Jane's is hilarious but so real that anyone infatuated with *Mad Men* and anyone who is interested in advertising and the 1960s must buy it and learn a lot while laughing. There have been many books on advertising. Some of them are good. Some are a bit snooty and exclusionary. Some are verrrrry self-important. But I have never read one that paints as honest and intimate and lively a picture of life in an agency at this important time in advertising history. Jane writes about the dramatic transition from the feudal period in advertising to the time of the creative revolution when the young took over culture. That was also the time when women were slowly—oh so slowly—being permitted to become stars. Jane writes about the difference in those periods, what happened along the way, and what the lasting impact has been on the advertising world we live in now. She is never boring. She isn't philosophic. She takes you to the scene. She captures famous personalities with truths that are awesome. She has great recall. This book tells it as it was.

Anyone who was in advertising at the same time as Jane will wonder, as I do, why I didn't know that there were such sexy agencies. Mine wasn't a sexy agency, I fear, because I was giddy with the thrill of making movies out of advertising commercials—and I was a dictator. Jane and the agencies she worked at made a lot of great advertising, but they managed to have fun, too. Or perhaps Jane's sense of humor is what keeps this book producing fun as well as an education.

God looking down, if He or She does look down, is happy with this book, I'd guess, because Jane does a scratchy job of painting the problems advertising women have had building respect, reputations, stardom, and stardom salaries. She is so clear at times on this subject that every man in advertising—and every client—will see the issue as if with 3-D glasses. But fellows, you won't be insulted. This book will give you new reasons to attack the old ways. And a good grudging laugh. When you have read it, you will want to give it to your daughters—even your clients' daughters.

You can see I liked it a lot. I did.

CHAPTER 1

A Day on Madison Avenue, 1967

"Was it really like that?"

As soon as people find out I actually worked at an advertising agency in the Mad Men *era, they pepper me with questions. "Was there really that much drinking?" "Were women really treated that badly?" And then they lean in and ask confidentially: "Was there really that much sex?"*

The answer is yes. And no. Mad Men *gets a lot of things right, but it gets some things wrong, too. So I thought I'd give you a typical day in my life on Madison Avenue in 1967, three years after I began working at Ogilvy & Mather as a copywriter.*

6:30 A.M. My husband, Michael, brings a cup of coffee to me in bed. It's a morning ritual and one of the many caring things he does for me. I know not many wives are so cosseted. "Don't ever mention this when we're with people from my office," he cautions me. "They'll think I'm henpecked."

He's not. We have a wonderful marriage—and a sexy one.

Michael is a former Marine Corps officer, crisply handsome, with just a bit of gray starting to show in his black hair. He attributes a recent promotion at his architectural firm to this premature streaking; he's now in charge of all building plans for New York Telephone, his firm's most important client. He stands beside the bed, already dressed in a blue Brooks Brothers suit, a white shirt (cuffs showing), and a bow tie. (Architects usually favor bow ties because they don't swing over drawings and smudge them.)

"You look very nice. Going to the office this early?"

"I'm inspecting a site on Staten Island. Want to meet for a drink after work?"

I light a cigarette, the first of the day. "Don't think I can. We're going to have casting calls all afternoon and I may not be able to leave by five."

"Well, try to be home in time for dinner. The girls miss you when you're not here." He bends down and kisses me. "So do I. Have a good day, Mops."

Mops is the family nickname for me. It's a shortened form of Mopsy, one of the rabbits in the Beatrix Potter nursery tales. Michael gave me the name when Kate was born. His mother read him the tales when he was a little boy, and I think he remembered incorrectly that Mopsy was the mother rabbit. It sounds like a maternal kind of name. I don't remember what the mother's name really was, but she was a good mother. I don't think I am. My priorities are job first, husband second, children third. It's the only way for a woman to survive in the advertising business. And in the marriage business.

I have a second cigarette with my coffee, then get up and check on my children. Kate, age eight, is in her room getting dressed in her Nightingale-Bamford school uniform: blue jumper, white short-sleeved blouse, and knee-high socks. She is a real moppet, blond and blue-eyed, quiet, introspective. In the next bedroom, Mabel, our live-in housekeeper, is supervising four-year-old Jenny. Jen is Kate's polar opposite: brown-haired, brown-eyed, noisy, exuberant. Mabel asks if I can drop Kate at Nightingale while she takes Jen to nursery school.

I have a second cup of coffee and another cigarette; I've already lost count.

8:15 A.M. I walk with Kate the few blocks from our apartment at 4 East Ninety-fifth Street to her school on Ninety-second Street between Madison and Fifth Avenues.

Kate reminds me that the school fashion show is at two o'clock today. "Are you coming to see me, Mommy?" I know that Kate is one of only a handful of girls chosen to show off fashions for the school fair. The outfits the girls will wear on-stage today will be sold at the Clotheshorse Booth tomorrow. It's a big deal for her, but I have a full day ahead of me at the office. "I don't think I can, darling. We have a ton of meetings today."

Kate is used to this. She is disappointed, but she doesn't protest. "I'll try," I offer. It doesn't sound convincing to Kate, who just keeps walking, her head down. It doesn't even sound convincing to me. But we're casting the Dove-for-Dishes commercial this afternoon. I have to be there.

We arrive at Nightingale-Bamford, one of the top girls'

schools in the city. I kiss Kate good-bye and watch her walk up the stairs to the landing, where the headmistress is greeting the girls, as she does every morning. Kate curtsys, as is the custom, she and the headmistress shake hands, as is also the custom, and she goes inside. I get on the Fifth Avenue bus and head downtown.

The Ogilvy & Mather advertising agency, where I am a copy supervisor, is at Forty-eighth Street and Fifth Avenue, convenient to Saks and St. Patrick's Cathedral, depending on whether you want to shop or pray. And within easy walking distance of Grand Central for the blue-blooded account guys (and they are all guys) who commute to Westport and environs.

There's a coffee shop next door to the office, and I stop in to pick up a cup. I'm at the front of the long line waiting to pay, and I spot an art director who works for me at the tail end. "Go on up, Doug. I'll get this." He motions his thanks. The male cashier beams at me. "Well, aren't you the nice little secretary to buy coffee for your boss. Hope he appreciates you."

Another day on Madison Avenue.

9:15 A.M. Everyone in the Gene Grayson creative group is here in their offices, except for Gene Grayson. He's the boss, so it's okay for him to come in later. The group consists of three copywriters, an art director, a television producer, a secretary, and me. I'm a copywriter, but I also supervise the others. We are housed along a corridor on the seventh floor. The writers and art director have small, windowless offices; the producer and I have slightly larger offices with one window; the secretary sits at a desk in the middle of the hallway. Gene, as copy group head, properly has the largest office of all, with *two* windows. As a vice president, he even rates a couch.

There's a reason why we have four writers and only one art director. This art director represents one of this agency's first tentative forays into the new "teamwork" school of creativity, where copywriters and art directors come up with the ideas together. Normally at Ogilvy & Mather, it's the writers who think up the television spots, then type the scripts and hand them over to the sketch men. We writers type the preliminary scripts on cheap yellow paper known as "copywriter roughs." The yellow paper is an old advertising tradition; it is supposed to signal to the writer that this is merely a rough draft so you can relax and be as creative as you like. I always wonder, though, why the paper is yellow, the color of cowardice.

We have some wonderful artists who sketch the visuals for the print ads or storyboards that we show our clients. One of our artists draws so charmingly that we all vie to have him do our storyboards; the clients usually okay them immediately. A client complained to me recently that the dog in the finished commercial wasn't grinning the way Wes had drawn him in the storyboard.

However, the new Doyle Dane Bernbach "team approach" is beginning to catch on at some of the smaller, less traditional agencies. Bill Bernbach decreed that at his agency, copywriters and art directors must work together on all advertising—even radio scripts. We hear that at DDB some art directors can't even draw. Imagine.

Our group has a lot of good writers. Scholarly, poetic Marianne, who has written sonnets about Good Seasons salad dressing and an ode to Milky Way. Pert, miniskirted Linda, who works on Maxim coffee. Witty Peter, who writes pornography in his spare time. Although Gene has promoted me to supervisor, I continue to write on all the accounts in our group.

We have several women writers because we work on "packaged goods"—the kind of products you find on supermarket shelves; the kind of products women are allowed to write ads for, like Dove soap, Drano, and Vanish toilet bowl cleaner. Down the hall, a creative group works on Mercedes-Benz; it is all male. One floor above us, another creative group handles the American Express card—all male. Only men are considered good enough to work on luxury accounts like Steuben Glass or liquor accounts like Rums of Puerto Rico. I'm told that at a rival agency, the chief copywriter on Kotex is a guy.

In addition to Peter, there are two other men in our group. Doug, the art director, represents the "new school." He doesn't draw all that well, but he's great at coming up with ideas. I'm not at all sure I like the new wave, though; I kind of preferred doing it all myself. Ken is our television producer, a silver-haired Brit who makes filming a commercial a wonderful experience. He believes that the talent performing in the spots *and* the creative people should travel first-class. With Ken, it was champagne and limousines all the way. I loved it, until he tried to seduce me late one night in the pool at the Beverly Hills Hotel.

9:30 A.M. My boss, copy group head Gene Grayson, arrives. (Officially, he is Eugene Debs Grayson; his parents named him in honor of the American Socialist.) Gene is intense, bearded, a brilliant advertising man. When he offered me the job at Ogilvy three years ago, at first I turned him down because I got cold feet about working as a copywriter when I didn't quite know what a copywriter did. "Listen, you little redheaded fink," he yelled at me over the phone, "come work for me and learn what advertising is all about. You may even write an ad someday." I capitulated.

There are several schools of advertising right now. There's the Doyle Dane school: tell it like it is, avoid hyperbole, have a little fun with the products. Ads like "Think small" for Volkswagen. "You don't have to be Jewish to like Levy's Jewish rye," for a bakery in Brooklyn, with ads that feature an Irish cop, an American Indian, a little Chinese boy. "We're only #2. We try harder" for Avis.

There's the David Ogilvy school: persuasive ads that often have long headlines and a lot of copy, packed with facts. D.O. is very proud of the first ad he wrote as the head of his tiny new agency. It was for Guinness Stout, and described in loving detail nine varieties of oyster that "taste their best when washed down with drafts of Guinness." He brags about using 3,242 words in an ad for the World Wildlife Fund.

And there's the Ted Bates school: hard-hitting, hard-sell advertising that drives the message home with powerful visuals and taglines repeated over and over. Hammers pounding on an animated head for Anacin; stomach acid bursting into flames for Tums. When people talk about how irritating advertising can be, it's usually this kind of work they have in mind.

Gene Grayson is a school unto himself. He specializes in mnemonic devices—usually a visual effect that helps the consumer remember your brand and what it stands for. For Maxim freeze-dried coffee he created the slogan "Turns every cup in your house into a percolator." A hand spoons in the Maxim, pours boiling water over the crystals, and stirs. Music sounds, the cup shimmers before your eyes, and—eureka!—the cup is suddenly transformed into a coffeepot, sitting there on your saucer. For Dove-for-Dishes, the campaign line is "I could have sworn I saw a dove fly into Mrs. So-and-So's window." The dove lands on the sink; there is a pinging sound, a flash of light, and—shazam!—the bird turns into a bottle of dishwashing liquid.

Now Gene stands at my office door, asking if I'm ready to leave for a meeting. Today is a big day for the agency and especially for me. The new president of our agency, Jim Heekin, has won a piece of business from Clairol. We are the only agency to chip away at the iron grip that Foote, Cone & Belding has had on the business for a zillion years. Our assignment: figure out the positioning and do the creative work for a new hair-coloring product. Heekin wanted the account assigned to Gene's group because he likes the commercials I have been writing for Dove-for-Dishes and wanted *me*. Am I ready? Never more so.

In the lobby of 2 East Forty-eighth Street, we meet Heekin and the account man who will supervise the Clairol business. There are only three women in account management in all of Ogilvy—all are lowly assistant account executives; all work on General Foods business. None is assigned to Clairol; it simply didn't occur to anyone.

At Clairol, the brand group for the new product greets us warmly. There are no women in brand management at Clairol, a company whose products are made exclusively for women.

We gather around a big conference table, the nine men and I, everybody lights a cigarette, and we begin. The project is so hush-hush that all of us from the agency have already signed confidentiality agreements.

The brand manager explains that today's meeting will be a short one, because the next step is for the agency's creative team to attend Clairol's hair-coloring academy to learn how to apply the product. He directs his next remark straight to me. "That's lovely red hair." I thank him. The Bergdorf beauty salon turned me into a redhead five years ago, but nobody at the agency knows that. The tagline for Clairol is "Does she . . . or doesn't she?" Coloring your hair was a topic even more personal than your sex life.

"A *very* lovely color," the brand manager persists.

Oh God, I think. *He knows.* "Thank you," I say again, lamely. There is a long silence. He is waiting. "It's Miss Clairol," I confess. And blush to my brown roots. My three agency colleagues look at me in astonishment. Jim Heekin, ever debonair, recovers first. "Why, Jane, how wonderful that you are using our client's product. And we never knew it." Gene Grayson looks at me with reproach; he will never again be able to call me a redheaded fink. The account man is shocked into silence. He is a conservative, serious, Bible-reading nondrinker, nonsmoker. He just gapes at me, the scarlet woman. The client, satisfied, beams at me.

11:30 A.M. Back at the agency, Gene asks if I am covering the casting auditions for my Dove commercial. All commercials are given names, and this one is called "Cupcake." It's a slice of life that opens with a youngish mother handing out cupcakes to her brood. A dove flies past her and into her neighbor's kitchen window. The mother bursts into the kitchen (in my Dove commercials, nobody ever knocks or rings a doorbell; they just rush in) and sees that damn bird turn into a bottle of dish soap. The neighbor declares that Dove keeps your hands soft and smooth, but the mother is doubtful. "With six kids and these dry hands, I need a miracle," she replies. By the end of the commercial, she is won over. "This Dove-for-Dishes *is* a miracle. I hope it comes in the giant economy size." The lawyers at Lever Brothers had trouble with that last line. They pointed out that there wasn't any "giant economy size" Dove bottle, so we couldn't refer to it. I argued that the mother in the commercial isn't stating a fact; she's simply expressing a hope. The lawyers backed down.

It's easy for me to write slices of life because I know how Americans talk. Before becoming an advertising copywriter, I was an associate producer for the quiz show *Name That Tune.* My job: interview the contestants and write their "spontaneous" dialogue with the master of ceremonies. Here's a sample. Emcee to Kansas Farmer's Wife: "What did your neighbors think about your being on our show?" Farmer's Wife: "George, there hasn't been this much excitement in town since our pig won second prize at the county fair."

I'm in the advertising business today because of the big quiz show scandal a few years ago. The most popular television programs then were quiz shows like *The $64,000 Question* and *Twenty One.* Charles Van Doren, with his long winning streak on *Twenty One,* became a national idol, even making the cover of *Time* magazine. Then news broke that the quiz shows were rigged and Van Doren confessed under oath that he was fed the answers in advance. Congress was so incensed that they ordered game shows off the air.

Overnight, *Name That Tune* was no more, and I was without a job. I needed the income to pay Mabel to look after the kids. Besides, I didn't want to stay home; I wanted to work. I knew there was something called "advertising," because we ran live commercials on the program. So I put together a few speculative ads and took my little portfolio to Ogilvy. That was when Gene offered me the job.

"Cupcake" is going to be a good commercial if the two actresses are just right, so casting is important. I have half an hour before the first audition; time to make "Mother Maas's Morning Rounds," a few minutes to check with the creative folks who report to me.

Marianne and Doug are in her office trying to think up a spot for Vanish. They are already working together in the Doyle Dane "copy/art team" fashion and Marianne tells me they spur each other on. We always have to make two versions of each Vanish commercial. During the day, when only women are presumed to be at home watching television, the networks allow us to call it a "toilet bowl" cleaner. At night, we have to refer to it as "bathroom bowl" cleaner. Apparently the word "toilet" is not appropriate for mixed company.

We have already given Vanish a positioning and a tagline: "Stuck with the nastiest job in the house? Make it Vanish." All the scrubbing brushes and sponges and scouring powder cans and bleach bottles disappear—whoosh!—and the housewife is left holding a container of Vanish. Now the assignment is to come up with the next commercial in the campaign. Marianne said they had an idea, a sort of takeoff on the kind of caper Lucy and Ethel might engage in on *I Love Lucy.* Two women would dress in suits of armor to attack the dreaded task. "It could be a funny spot," Doug suggests, with a question mark in his voice. I'm not so sure about it, either, and I ask them to show me a few more ideas.

In the next office, Peter is working on a subway campaign for Ammens medicated powder. He envisions a series of posters with funny illustrations of situations that call for a soothing sprinkle of Ammens. He shows me a rough sketch of an old-fashioned corset with the headline "A lady on this train has a corset that's killing her." It's eye-catching, but I question whether any women these days wear corsets. Peter rolls his eyes. "It's hyperbole, for God's sake. Sure, we could show a girdle, but that would be just plain ugly. Even the word 'corset' is funny."

I suspect Peter is right. Of all the writers in our group, he has a flair for writing comedy. "Let's show it to Gene tomorrow," I agree.

Linda and I arrive at her office at the same time. "I just had a haircut with Emil," she explains. Emil is our in-house barber, installed by David Ogilvy when he started the agency. "And while I was sitting in the chair, David Ogilvy arrived. Emil had forgotten he had an appointment and gave the time slot to me. Poor Emil was so upset he dropped his scissors, but Mr. Ogilvy told him to go right on cutting my hair, and he sat down and chatted with me. He was charming."

D.O. was famous for his lack of patience. "Oh God, Linda. How long did you keep him waiting?"

"Oh, Emil never cut *his* hair. Once he finished me, Mr.

Ogilvy remembered he had a meeting and had to leave, too. But on the way out, he said he'd seen me at his Magic Lantern presentation last week, and asked me how I liked it."

"What did you tell him?"

"I told him Magic Lanterns were pretty boring, but I thought *he* was divine. He's a very sexy man, isn't he?"

"Oh God."

Magic Lanterns are a tool D.O. invented to teach creative people what works, what doesn't, and why in various advertising categories. They are slide presentations that lay out certain "rules." The first one he wrote was "How to Create Advertising That Sells." Others became more specific. "How to Advertise Travel" exhorts us to "show the natives, not the tourists" and not to be afraid of long copy. "How to Create Food Advertising That Sells" tells us how to talk to women. David, despite his early career as a chef, clearly thinks only women are involved with food preparation. The rules in this Lantern include "Tell her how and when to use your product" and "Don't forget to tell her it tastes good."

Lanterns are powerful new business tools. David turns them into ads that run in *The New York Times.* In addition to touting all the success we have achieved for clients, the ads always end with a statement that these guidelines are merely a small sample of what the agency knows about selling the category. The rest is confidential and strictly reserved for clients of Ogilvy & Mather. Every time one of these ads runs, prospective new clients appear.

"Linda, I'm actually glad you think Magic Lanterns are boring. David Ogilvy has just assigned Gene and me to write the newest one—'What O&M Knows About Selling Packaged Goods.' And just to make sure that it's entertaining, we are assigning *you* to write the first draft."

12 noon. The Ogilvy casting department is on the eleventh floor. The lobby is already full of sleek young women who've come to read for the Dove commercial. Ogilvy's casting directors work hard to discover new talent; they go to all the Broadway, Off Broadway, and even Off-Off Broadway shows. Other agencies often simply "line up the usual suspects"; the reason you see so many familiar faces cropping up in commercial after commercial. We always ask the talent if they are in any spots that are currently running, or if they have ever appeared in a commercial for a competing product. Yes to either question rules them out.

Each audition takes about ten minutes. It's important to be polite to the actresses; today's nobody may be tomorrow's superstar, and we want the agency to have a reputation for class befitting our founder. But I can tell who is wrong for the part before they say a word. For instance, I don't want to cast a cute blonde who looks about eighteen years old as the mother of six kids. We exchange some niceties with the actresses and ask each one to read the script. After the first few readings, my own words starts to sound flat and boring.

Suddenly, there's electricity. An actress named Mary Jo Catlett enters. She is pleasingly plump, probably in her thirties, and tells us she is playing the soubrette role in the Broadway revival of *Hello, Dolly! w*ith Carol Channing. She certainly looks the part, but can she act? It turns out that indeed she can. She is perfect: wistful, frazzled, funny, believable. And, wonder of wonders, she has never appeared in a commercial before. I know we will have to invite her back to do a second reading for Gene Grayson and the client, but I'm already sure she's my "Cupcake" mom.

I look at my watch. Twenty after one. If I take a taxi, I can make it up to Nightingale in time for the fashion show. We aren't going to see anybody better than Mary Jo; the producer and the casting director can take over for the next hour; nobody will miss me. In the taxi, though, I feel horribly guilty about leaving the auditions.

1:55 P.M. They save the first few rows in the auditorium for the parents of girls in the show. Most seats are already taken, all by mothers; there isn't one father present. I sit down in the very first row just as the show begins. First grade. Second grade. Then out comes Kate, in a blue party dress with a blue bow in her hair, looking like Alice in Wonderland. The audience breathes a quiet "ooooh." Kate spots me and gives a big smile of surprise and delight. The rest of her performance is only for me. She twirls slowly, as someone has instructed her, to show off the full skirt, curtsys to the audience, smiles at me again, and exits to applause. I last through fourth grade. When the fifth grader comes on, dressed in a party gown, the teacher at the piano plays a few bars of "Hello, Dolly!" and I think of the auditions I'm missing. I slink out, now feeling guilty about leaving without going backstage to hug Kate, but more guilty about staying. "I'm in a real hurry," I tell the taxi driver. "I have a casting session."

3:10 P.M. The casting session is over. They have selected one other finalist for the part of the mother, and two additional actresses for the other role. I'm back in my office, at my typewriter, when the chairman of the agency, John Elliott Jr., known as Jock, appears in my doorway. "I stopped in about an hour ago, but you were probably having a late lunch."

Embarrassed, I confess that I was watching my daughter perform at a school event. Jock beams approval. "We should encourage all the mothers at Ogilvy to give their children high priority. Come to think of it, we should encourage the *fathers,* too. But I am here on official agency business. It is my great pleasure to tell you that at our board of directors meeting today, you were elected a vice president. As you know, only one other woman here has that title. Congratulations!" We shake hands solemnly, then Jock makes his distinctive formal bow and leaves.

Lots of men at Ogilvy are vice presidents. An account man I work with went recently to Jim Heekin to complain that he had not yet been given the title. "But John," Jim reasoned, "*everybody* is a vice president." "Exactly," John said. He was soon elected. The title doesn't come with a raise or a promotion in rank; it's simply an indication that the agency values you. You become an officer of the company. As Jock said, only one other woman is a vice president: Reva Korda, second in command to the creative head of the agency.

Ogilvy & Mather is a male preserve, as most agencies are, but there are a few men who champion the promotion of women. Jock is one of them. He was taught early by his suffragette mother that women could do anything they set their minds to. I admire Jock's wife, Elly, who is on the boards of Barnard (her alma mater) and New York Hospital. At Ogilvy, Jock is the biggest supporter we women have.

David Ogilvy says that he believes in hiring "ladies and gentlemen" with brains, but he seems dubious about women and careers. In his book *Confessions of an Advertising Man*—the bestselling book about advertising ever written—D.O. described his rule against nepotism. If two Ogilvy employees marry, David wrote, one of them must leave, preferably the woman, "to stay home and raise her babies." As far as I know, we are the only agency that has this regulation. D.O.'s partners are trying to persuade him to soften on this position, but today, in the liberated 1960s, it is still in effect.

I reach for the phone to call Michael and tell him the news, but it's already ringing. Reva Korda is calling to congratulate me. "If I didn't like you so much, I would probably resent you at this moment," she says candidly. Reva has been the lone female at the top for a few years now; it must be hard for her to share the spotlight. I know she wanted the Clairol assignment in her domain, so that's another blow. After we hang up, I ponder her words.

My phone rings again. It's Nick Evans, CEO of the Drackett Company, makers of Vanish and Drano. He's just seen my "Crying Plumber" commercial. The premise is that new Liquid Drano "keeps your drains so clean you may never need a plumber." So the actor playing the plumber cries throughout the entire thirty seconds. "I love it," Nick says. "I hope you win a ton of awards."

Another phone call. Jim Heekin. This is really my day, I

think; two presidents within two minutes. "Bad news," Jim says. "As soon as Lever heard we got the Clairol assignment, they called to tell me it was a major conflict. We have to resign Clairol or they'll move all their business." He didn't have to remind me that Lever Brothers was our biggest client. "It was nice working with you on Clairol . . . for about twenty minutes." He pauses. "By the way, there's something I've been meaning to ask you since this morning. What color is your hair in real life?" "Red," I say firmly, and we both laugh.

The second we hang up, the phone rings again. Heekin a second time. "I forgot to say congratulations on your vice presidency."

Gene arrives to give me a hug. "The whole group is taking you out for drinks tonight. No excuses that you need to entertain Michael's clients or get home to the kids. This is a big deal for the people who report to you." I agree, feeling guilty. I don't spend enough time with the creative group outside of office hours.

Finally, I get to call Michael and tell him my news. He is quietly very pleased. "How about taking me out for dinner tonight?" he teases. I remind him that it's Friday, and Mabel always likes to leave by six to go home to her family in Brooklyn for the weekend. "And the gang wants to buy me a drink to celebrate. So could you get home on the early side?"

"Sure. I know you need to do this. Have fun," Michael says, "but don't stay out too late." I hang up, feeling guiltier than ever. I don't spend enough time with my family. I think that I'm lucky to have Michael, a man other women lust after, and the kind of marriage other couples envy. So far, in our ten years of marriage, we have disagreed about only two things: dogs and golf.

I kept begging Michael for a dog. "You grew up with a dog; I grew up with a dog," I'd whine. "Not in a New York apartment," Michael always said firmly. After Kate was born, I stepped up my pleas, but Michael was firmer than ever. "No dog in a New York apartment." After Jenny was born, I thought the time had come for us to try for a boy. "What do you think about a third child?" I asked Michael. His answer: "How would you like a poodle?"

Golf was another matter. Michael adored the game, played every chance he got and wanted me to play, too, so we would "have something to do together in our golden years." I did eighteen holes in the 150s or 160s, playing through the rough the whole way. It wasn't a sport for me; it was jungle warfare. After about five years of this battering, I sat Michael down one night, took a deep breath, and spit out the bad news. "I'm not going to play golf anymore." "That's wonderful, Mops," Michael said. "You're so awful at it, I didn't know why you kept trying."

4:15 P.M. I'm at my desk trying to write copy for Maxim coffee, but my heart isn't in it. I'm too excited about the promotion. A shadow falls over my typewriter and I turn to find David Ogilvy standing there in my office. He wrote in *Confessions* that he never summoned people to his office; he believed it terrified them. Instead, he went to their offices. Clearly, he has no idea how heart-stopping it is to have him materialize before you.

Michael and Jane Maas after their marriage in 1957.

"Hi, Mr. Ogilvy," I manage.

"My dear girl, I have just screened that commercial with the plumber. I absolutely loathe it. That overweight actor blubbering away." My stomach lurches. "But I want to congratulate you on the eccentric casting. Brilliant."

"Thank you, Mr. Ogilvy."

"One thing more. As of today, you are the only vice president of this agency who calls me 'Mister.' So you must stop it immediately. Congratulations." He shakes my hand warmly.

"Thank you," I say again, and stop. I can't quite utter the word "David."

5:15 P.M. We all gather at Rattazzi's, the Ogilvy hangout right across the street from the office. Because it's fairly early, we manage to snag a big table in the dimly lighted rear. Each of us orders a different drink; it's a sort of personality test. Gene has a double scotch on the rocks; worldly Linda has a martini, very dry; literary Marianne a sherry; curious Peter a drink I've never heard of called a Negroni. Ken, our Brit, asks for a Pimm's Cup but they don't stock it; I can't hear what he mutters as a substitute. Doug and I are the only wine drinkers; he Chianti, I Soave. I open my second pack of cigarettes.

5:50 P.M. The party is in full swing. I really would like a second glass of wine, but it's not fair to Michael and the girls. I try to leave unnoticed, and it's easier than I expected; most people are well into their second round. Only Gene spots me and escorts me to the door. I kiss him on the cheek. "Thank you for making this happen." He makes a face. "*You* made it happen." I walk over to Madison and take the bus uptown. Two taxis today were enough.

6:35 P.M. The door to our apartment has a makeshift poster—four eight-by-ten sheets of typing paper taped together—that says CONGRATULATIONS, VP MOPS.

Michael, Kate, and Jenny are already eating dinner. Hugs, kisses, applause. Mabel's meat loaf is warm and waiting in the oven; Michael pours me a glass of wine, that second glass I've been wanting. I'm so glad to be home; it's been a long week, and today was a long day. The telephone rings and Kate runs to answer it. "Mr. Grayson," she announces. It's a familiar name in our household. Michael raises his eyebrows; it means *Do you really have to take the call?* I shrug apologetically; how can I not?

"Sorry to intrude," Gene says, "but I came back here to the office to clean up some paperwork." Guilt overwhelms me. Gene is working late, and I'm home. "And there was a message from the Drackett folks. They are going ahead with the Industrial-Strength Drano project, and they need a copywriter there for the lab tour on Monday. I just talked to Peter and he can fly out on Sunday."

"But Marianne's been doing all the work on Drackett. It's really her—"

"*Industrial-Strength* Drano," Gene interrupts me. "Really not a girl's account. And, anyway, Peter is all set. He said he was supposed to write the Dove copy over the weekend, but since he's traveling on Sunday, I didn't think it was fair to make him work Saturday, too. I said you'd write it." Pause. "Or I would."

I don't hesitate for a second. "Oh, I can write it. I'll have it for you Monday first thing."

Back at the dinner table, both my daughters look at me with resignation. "Mommy, do you have to work this weekend?" Kate asks.

"I just have to work *one* of the days. Tell you what: tomorrow, we'll have a picnic lunch in Central Park and then maybe Daddy will take us rowing." Michael looks sheepish. "What?" I ask him.

"I promised I'd play golf tomorrow." I try not to let Kate and Jenny see that I'm disappointed and mutter something about Daddy working hard and needing some time for himself. I ask him if he is going all the way to Pine Valley. That golf club is a cherished enclave of male bonding, where golfers with hangovers can order the breakfast specialty of the house, a milk punch laced with bourbon. Oh, no, he tells me; Pine Valley is only for overnight outings. Pine Valley, in fact, is *next* weekend. I wince. Michael realizes he has given me news he didn't intend to reveal quite yet, and grins at me. I grin back. He always wins me over.

10:15 P.M. Michael and I are in bed. We have all agreed to a plan for the weekend and everyone seems happy. Tomorrow, Michael will play golf, and I'll take the girls to the playground in the morning and write copy in the afternoon. Sunday will be a family day.

"When will I get to visit the Pine Valley Club with you?" I ask sleepily.

There is a pause. "I don't think you really want to visit Pine Valley."

"Of course I do. You always describe it as the be-all, end-all. Why shouldn't I want to spend a weekend there, too?"

"They don't have a ladies' room."

CHAPTER 2

Sex in the Office

The fictional Sterling Cooper agency of *Mad Men* is supposed to be based on the real Young & Rubicam, which was indeed located on Madison Avenue at Fortieth Street. Women who worked there in the sixties confided to me that more sex went on in that agency than on the television show. "It was in the air," one woman said. "You breathed it."

Joan Lipton is one of the grandes dames of advertising, a tiny but steely Queen Mother type, one of the first women to have her name on the door of an agency. So I was a bit reluctant to broach the topic of office sex, but I had to ask that obligatory question. I knew she started her career as a copywriter at Y&R. "Was there much sex in the office?" She was quick to answer. "Of course people were partaking," she said, "but you have to understand that at the time I was married, had a three-year-old child, and was living in Connecticut."

"Then were you *aware* of much sexual activity?" I pressed.

"Aware?" Joan sniffed. "Heavens, I *partook*."

Copywriter Linda Bird Francke (who later worked for me

at Ogilvy) also started at Y&R, but she wasn't yet even a beginning copywriter. "I was in the typing pool, and I lost my virginity to the account executive on Jell-O. He was immensely charming, a Hungarian who had been a professional soccer star, came over here to play a game, and managed to defect. I was smitten. He took me to his apartment one evening after work and we had sex. Then his telephone rang, and I could hear a woman crying and accusing him of being unfaithful.

"Pretty soon after that I figured out he was working his way through the typing pool. So somebody or other in the pool was always crying because she suspected he was sexually involved with somebody else. And she—whichever one she happened to be—was always right."

According to eyewitnesses at Y&R, lots of sex also went on *outside* the office. The single guys, like the Hungarian account executive, had apartments in the city. The more senior guys, who turned out to be the real swingers, usually had homes in Westport or Scarsdale, with wives stashed away in them. So the Hotel Lexington became a favorite trysting spot. It was just a few blocks from the agency, and the front desk clerks didn't raise an eyebrow when you asked for a key at noon and returned it at two. If you met fellow staff members coming through the lobby, you simply averted your eyes.

Why was sex so rampant, so flagrant, so delicious? For one thing, the Pill had just been approved (in 1960), and doctors were writing out prescriptions for single women as well as for married ones. So women didn't have to worry so much about getting pregnant. It's hard to imagine today what a nightmare a possible pregnancy was—the words "I'm late" were the thunderclap of doom. Abortions were not only illegal but considered shameful, and most doctors simply didn't perform them. Of course, we had all heard the horror stories of quacks and back-alley procedures in dirty offices, but even these illegal guys were hard to find. I considered myself quite a sophisticated New York woman in the mid-sixties, but when a young friend got pregnant and came to me for help, I didn't know a single doctor to suggest. I had to turn to my brother-in-law, writer Peter Maas. Swinging bachelors like Peter often knew what to do and where to go. Peter did.

The term "sexual harassment" hadn't been invented yet, or certainly wasn't in our vocabularies. Most women then working in advertising were either secretaries or copywriters, and 99 percent of us had male bosses. The boss was in control of your salary, your raise, your career advancement . . . your life. If he wanted to go to bed with you, you had to ask yourself what mattered more: your self-respect or your career.

A number of people confided recently that *women* were sometimes the ones doing the seducing. The best way to get promoted from secretary to copywriter was for your boss to make it happen. And the fastest way to make that happen was to make it with your boss. One woman who wanted to be a writer worked briefly for me as a secretary at Ogilvy, then moved to another agency to be administrative assistant to the vice chairman. She was swiftly promoted to copywriter. Ultimately, after his messy divorce, the vice chairman married her. Doing research for this book, I asked her if she remembered there being much sex in the office. She looked at me in surprise. "How do you think I got Joe?"

Some women were outwardly cynical about sex in general and sex in the office in particular. Joan Holloway, *Mad Men*'s seductive office manager, gives some practical advice to newcomer secretary Peggy Olson. "Peggy, this isn't China. There's no money in virginity." A fellow copywriter at Ogilvy had a similar attitude. She came to my office one morning to tell me she had begun divorce proceedings. "It's so *relaxing* to be able to go to bed with anybody I want and not feel guilty about it." She put a persuasive hand on my arm. "*You* should get a divorce."

It was socially acceptable for men, single or married, to have affairs. It was even okay, in that freewheeling era, for a woman, even a married woman, to have an affair, as long as it was considered serious. But openly promiscuous women were punished in one way or another. One notorious sexual encounter actually occurred *inside* an agency—Young & Rubicam again. Late one night, an account man was having sex with his secretary. He was fairly junior, so his inside office didn't have a door, and the big boss happened to be working late and caught them. Result: the account guy was promoted and got an office with a door; the secretary was fired.

Some account men faced certain occupational hazards. They were the ones who had to show up on the set of commercials being filmed for their clients' brands, and therefore needed to steel themselves against the considerable charms of the actresses appearing in the spots. At Ogilvy, at least two of our senior men fell in love with actresses, divorced their wives, and married their paramours. One marriage lasted; one didn't. So much for show business.

Another occupational hazard for account men was procuring for clients. One man, now a respected client of mine, told me of his early days as a brand-new account executive at Dancer

Fitzgerald Sample. "One of the most conservative, most WASPy agencies on the planet," he said.

"A client was coming in from out of town and he telephoned me to fix him up with a date. I told him I'd check some of my ex-girlfriends for availability. 'Not a date,' the client said. 'A *date.*' I could hear the italics in his voice. I had no idea what to do, so I rushed off to the senior partner. 'This sort of thing may occur at other agencies,' he said icily, 'but it does not go on at Dancer Fitzgerald Sample.'

"Now I was really panicked, so I went to an art director in the agency. I figured creative guys would have the scoop. He said, 'Oh sure, this happens all the time.' And he told me to go to the newsstand in the lobby and buy a copy of *Screw* magazine; all the hookers advertise in it.

"It took me two or three tries before I had the nerve to ask the young woman at the stand for *Screw.* First I bought a pack of gum. Then I bought a pack of cigarettes—and I didn't even smoke. Finally I bought the magazine.

"Well, it was loaded with personals and pretty explicit invitations for 'dates.' So, being a good account man, and wanting to assure my client of the best, I telephoned four or five of the young ladies, interviewed them, and made careful notes. One sounded a bit too downscale for my client to take to dinner. Another was too overtly sexual. I zeroed in on a girl named Judy, made an appointment to meet her, went to her apartment, and prepaid the two hundred dollars. We even shook hands on the deal. I put the magazine away and forgot about it.

"The client called to say he was pleased. I figured that project was completed.

"A few weeks later, I told my wife that my Friday paycheck

was in my briefcase, as usual. I heard a shriek. 'You bastard,' she yelled at me. 'You lousy, two-timing bastard.' She stood there with the copy of *Screw* magazine, folded open to the page with all those telephone numbers circled. And all my notations, like 'Too rough' and 'Promising.'

"I tried to explain what had happened. 'I did it for a client.' 'Aha!' she said. 'So you're not only a bastard, you're a pimp.' To this day, I'm not sure whether she believed me. Or just forgave me."

For really fervent extramarital affairs, finances often became an issue. An account supervisor at J. Walter Thompson told me his sad story. Jim was having a torrid affair with a copywriter, but they were both married. His wife and kids were in Scarsdale; her husband worked, but her children and the housekeeper were at her New York apartment during the day. So every time he and Barbara got together, he had to book a hotel room. They wanted to be together a lot, so it was getting expensive.

He complained to a friend at another agency who had been in the same predicament. The friend had solved it by renting a tiny studio apartment in Greenwich Village. It was still a bit expensive, he admitted. Maybe Jim would like to share the apartment and the rent. Jim agreed immediately, sight unseen.

The day the key arrived in the office mail, he and Barbara bought a bottle of wine for the housewarming and took a taxi down to Perry Street. They opened the door and discovered the other couple already at play. The men had neglected to work out their signals.

The next time they went to the apartment, the coast was clear, but Barbara said the place was so filthy she refused to stay in it for a single minute. Jim had to take her out for lunch. The third time, they went down with mops and buckets, bleach and detergent. It still felt dirty to her, so they devoted yet another lunch hour to cleaning up. Jim's wife was puzzled. "Your hands look so red and rough. If I didn't know better, I'd swear you were doing housework."

They actually managed to make love in the apartment a few times, but Barbara never liked it. She said she could never be entirely sure the sheets were clean, and it made her uncomfortable. She always wanted to hurry things up and get out of there.

The apartment ruined their sex life and ended the romance.

J. Walter Thompson was probably the most conservative of the big agencies. They didn't pay very well (none of the big agencies did at that time), and it was ruled with an iron hand for some fifty years by Stanley Resor. There wasn't much sex at JWT because most of the offices didn't have doors. This was supposedly by order of Mrs. Resor, who had been a copywriter and knew what went on at agencies. Word was out that if you went to work at Thompson, you had to take a vow of chastity, poverty, and obedience.

I was a copywriter and then a creative director at Ogilvy & Mather for twelve years, from 1964 to 1976. Was there much sex going on? At the time I would have said no, absolutely not. Now, looking back, I would say yes, there was a lot of sex, but it was more *discreet* at Ogilvy than at other agencies. It was more *gentlemanly.* A secretary having an affair with her boss would address him as "Mister" during office hours. He, in turn, would be careful to flirt chivalrously with other secretaries, but never with her. The entire agency knew what was going on, but we never said a word. After all, we had *ethics*.

David Ogilvy set the standard for discretion. I was having drinks one evening with his good friend and copy chief, who may have had one martini too many. "Mr. Ogilvy is certainly attractive," I said. (I was still calling him "Mr. Ogilvy" at this point). "But he never seems to stray. Does he ever—" The copy chief interrupted me. "David is one of the great swordsmen of the Western world."

David appreciated beauty and first-class quality, whether it was in an advertisement or in a woman. One of his many strict rules was that no Ogilvy & Mather employee was allowed to appear in any of our advertisements. He relaxed that rule just twice. The first time it was for Angelique, an eighteen- or nineteen-year-old intern from the Caribbean who was spending the summer at the agency to learn about advertising. Angelique was breathtaking, burnished bronze, a young Josephine Baker. A few days after she joined us, a memo went out from David announcing an exception to the rule about employees in advertisements; if any of us wanted to feature Angelique, it was okay.

At the end of the summer, I interviewed Angelique for the agency newsletter. She told me she and D.O. had met only once, fleetingly, at the welcoming reception for interns. She was surprised and flattered by his generosity, she could have used the money, but there had been no offers for ads or commercials, and now she was headed back to college. I remember the incident simply as a tribute to beauty by a Renaissance courtier.

My friend Ken Roman wrote the insightful and definitive biography of D.O. titled *The King of Madison Avenue.* Ken, as an account man and ultimately chairman of Ogilvy, worked closely with David for twenty-six years, and then spent two years in intensive research on his subject before sitting down to write. Roman says that David Ogilvy was full of paradoxes: "A model of good taste, he often behaved like a spoiled child in restaurants and regularly told a joke about farting."

I had been at Ogilvy & Mather for less than a week when I saw David coming down the hall of the ninth floor. "Mr. Ogilvy," I said. "I'm Jane Maas, your newest copywriter." David raised his eyebrows. "Well, newest copywriter, why aren't you writing?" And he gave a little wave of dismissal, indicating that I should hurry back to my office posthaste and type away. Then he smiled at me, and I was enthralled.

David was a master of body language. After delivering any major speech, he would make a slight upward gesture with his hands outstretched. It never failed to prompt a standing ovation. Every year for the twelve years I was there, D.O. stood up at the agency's annual Christmas meeting to announce that every man jack of us—including the kid in the mailroom hired yesterday—would receive a one-hundred-dollar bonus. Every year he made that upward gesture, and every year I led the tribute, leaping from my front-row seat and applauding. (A large part of my success is due simply to the fact that I'm short, so wherever I am, I always try to sit down front. It's a huge advantage, because in addition to seeing better, you are also *seen.*)

David was married three times. I knew only the attractive, vibrant Herta, decades younger than he, with whom he spent the last years of his life, most of it at his Château de Touffou, near Poitiers. In the spring of 1974, learning that Michael, our daughters, and I were going to spend a month in France, on the coast of Brittany, David sent me a note asking us "to dine and spend the night." As we drove toward Poitiers, Jenny asked if we were going to stay in a "real castle." Michael told her not to be disappointed. "Many people call their home a 'château' when really it is just a large house with many rooms."

We approached Touffou, with its eleventh-century keep, fifteenth-century Renaissance wing, battlements and moat, and former jousting yard the size of two football fields. "My God," Michael said, "it *is* a castle." David stood on the central balcony, waving us in. He was elated to have as a guest an architect who would fully appreciate the glories of the château, and he took Michael on a tour that covered every inch of the place. Touffou had been declared a "national treasure" by France and therefore special artisans had to be called in whenever repairs were needed. D.O. grumbled that every time the roof leaked, it took all of *his* national treasure to fix it.

Herta confided in me that the grounds and gardens and vineyard were her husband's special love, and he employed a small army of gardeners. Yet in this immense château, there was only one maid and no cook. Herta did the cooking. It was another David paradox: he could be immensely generous on one score, miserly on another.

By late afternoon, the Maas château tour had progressed to David's treasured gardens and superbly manicured croquet lawn. He discovered that Michael was a first-class croquet player, a member of the elite Westhampton Mallet Club, and challenged him to a match. David won the first round, and called to Herta, "You must come and watch. This is the best croquet player we have ever had at Touffou." They played again, and this time Michael won. Thirsting for revenge, D.O. invited us to stay for another day. We could not, and when we drove away the next morning, the lord of the manor waved good-bye from the balcony, brandishing a croquet mallet. "Come back soon." We never got back to Touffou, but David remembered those two matches. When he was inducted into the Advertising Hall of Fame, I went up to congratulate him at the reception. "Herta," he said to his wife, "you remember Jane, don't you? She's married to the croquet player."

One of my favorite memories of David Ogilvy is the day when the agency opened its cafeteria, a longtime dream of his. It was a big day, and the place was packed. He spotted me as we were about to enter the line for salads, and whispered urgently, "Don't leave me. I don't know anybody. You know everybody. Stay with me." We selected our salads and reached the cashier. Like royalty, D.O. carried no money. I paid. Like royalty, he never repaid me.

But back to David Ogilvy as sex object. He was apparently, like Julius Caesar, a man who continued on best terms with former loves. Herta Ogilvy graciously invited both of the previous wives to his big memorial service in New York and the reception afterward. Both accepted. I watched the three women chatting together cordially, and wondered whether other women in that gathering were nursing a special, private grief.

Not all Ogilvy events were discreet. Some of our parties became famous for sex and booze. The Lever party, just before Christmas, was one. It was a big bash, always at a Midtown hotel, hosted by the Lever Brothers account group to thank all the people who had worked on their business during the year. The clients weren't invited, though; just the agency people, with a heavy tilt on the invitation list toward secretaries. The party started around five in the afternoon and went on with nonstop drinking, usually until the next morning. Because it was in a hotel, couples could easily slip off to a room together.

The General Foods account group at Ogilvy also threw a big annual party, but this one was more restrained because clients were invited. The Ogilvy account men couldn't get roaring drunk because they had to entertain their guests, and the Ogilvy creative folks wanted to stay sober and impress the GF bigwigs. Ken Roman, then head of the GF account group, was proud of the party. "It's the *nicest* one of all, don't you think?" he asked me. I had to admit it was the most decorous.

One year, the party went on later than usual, and one of my favorite General Foods clients offered to drop me off at my apartment building on his way back to Westport. He politely waited in his car to see me safely inside, but I had forgotten my keys. Michael was away, Mabel and the girls were at our summer rental in Westhampton, and there was no night doorman. Dave took me home to Connecticut, where his wife greeted me warmly, loaned me a nightgown, gave me a toothbrush, and behaved as though this happened all the time.

I bumped into Ken the next day at the office. "The party was a bit raucous last night," he said with a worried frown, "and it went on much later than usual. What time did *you* get home?" "I never did get home," I told him. "I went to Westport with Dave." Ken just groaned. I had ruined the reputation of the General Foods party.

It was said that no virgin ever returned a virgin from the Ogilvy boat ride, the wildest event of all. It was a cruise around Manhattan Island, to which everyone at the agency was invited. This annual affair was an orgy of heavy drinking and fairly overt sex. At least it *was* annual, until the office manager got so drunk on one cruise that he fell overboard. He was fished out, none the worse for wear, but Ogilvy management weighed anchor on the boat ride.

In his wickedly funny book *From Those Wonderful Folks Who Gave You Pearl Harbor,* Jerry Della Femina writes of the famous party held yearly at his agency, then Della Femina Travisano & Partners. It was a sex contest. And that's just what they called it: "the Sex Contest." They took a blind vote to name the person at the agency you'd most like to go to bed with. First prize was a weekend at the Plaza Hotel; second prize was one night at the Plaza; third prize was a night on the couch in Jerry's office. Jerry says people at his place really got into the spirit of the thing. One shy girl in accounting Xeroxed her breasts and hung pictures of them on the walls. A very attractive woman executive put a sexy photo of herself in the men's room, on the wall a man would be facing. The caption under her picture read: "May I help you with that?" Jerry hastens to add that it was really all fun; only one couple in the fifteen years of the contest actually collected the prize.

Office parties were one threat to marital fidelity; location shoots were another. They were generally in Los Angeles or on some remote Caribbean island. There you were, a million miles from your spouse and your kids, staying at some hotel like the

Beverly Hills, with Jacuzzis and terry-cloth robes and room service. Shooting a commercial for two or three days gets to be a very intimate experience because everyone is thrown together for twelve or fifteen hours a day. What you're doing is so important that the rest of the world recedes, and the production becomes your whole universe. It's like being in a lifeboat.

Philip Roth gets it right in *Everyman,* the only one of his novels with an advertising agency background. His protagonist, the Everyman of the title, goes off to a shoot on a tropical isle, where he begins a passionate affair with a beautiful model. The romance leads to a bitter divorce and dark days. Philip never worked at an agency, but his older brother, Sandy Roth, was a talented art director/creative director at Ogilvy. Philip is known for doing very careful research for his books, whether it's about kosher butcher shops or advertising agencies. I'm sure he got some of his details from Sandy; I know he got a few from me. Philip and I were students together at Bucknell University and have been friends for more than fifty years. While he was writing *Everyman,* he'd call me occasionally and ask, "Could it happen like this at an agency?" or "Would they have dialogue like this?"

I remember going to only two location shoots, but neither of them was very sexy. The first was for Whistle Spray Cleaner. We licensed the Disney music "Whistle While You Work" and gave the product the tagline "Makes everything in your house as clean as a . . . well, why do you think we called it Whistle?" The commercial I wrote took place in a busy restaurant, where the leading lady was sprinting about, spraying Whistle on dirty surfaces. We rented a nondescript restaurant in the Bronx for a day.

The storyboard called for a man to be at the pay telephone, fumble unsuccessfully for a piece of paper, then write a telephone number on the white wall. He turned to the telephone, and the whistling woman came by, sprayed, and wiped. When he turned back to the wall, his number was gone. I asked the young actor to do a big double take. "I can do a *triple* take," he said. "In five seconds?" I scoffed. "Watch me," he said.

His name was F. Murray Abraham, and that was the first commercial he made, on his road to Hollywood and the Academy Award for Best Actor for his role in *Amadeus.* Whenever he comes to New York to appear on Broadway, I go backstage to say hello, and we reminisce about Whistle.

Another location shoot was for Vanish toilet bowl cleaner. I had to go to Los Angeles for the filming. Michael couldn't believe it. "Do they have better toilet bowls in California?" The reason was that we were using a newly invented technique called "humanation," and we needed to go to its source. "Humanation" was a kind of three-dimensional animation in which an object is turned into a person or an animal. For Vanish, we had come up with the idea of calling it "the angry bowl cleaner" that gets fighting mad at stains. Every time anyone used Vanish, the container would turn into a lion and roar at the camera. It was an awful commercial and I still shudder when I think of it.

For the shoot, we rented an old mansion in the hills above the city. The ancient air conditioners roared louder than the lion, so they had to be turned off while we were filming. By mid-morning, all of us were sweating like pigs. Our diminutive star, an unknown young actor named Arte Johnson, was losing weight by the minute. "My mother always told me that

Hollywood was hell," he complained. "And she was right." Arte became one of the mainstays of television's hit show *Laugh-In,* playing the Nazi with the helmet who rode the tricycle and fell over.

There was one location shoot, however, that did have serious consequences, and I was indeed involved in it, although indirectly. The copywriter and the art director reported to me, and had been working together for months with no apparent sparks flying. On location in California for Dove-for-Dishes, they stayed at a hotel that offered the latest sexual fad—water beds. This proved so seductive that they returned to New York with the announcement that they were going to be married. All well and good, except that the lady in question, the copywriter, already had a husband.

My involvement? The spot wasn't very good; the team had devoted most of their talents to the water bed and not to the commercial. The client despised it, and it never ran. I received a temporary demotion. To demonstrate to the client, Lever Brothers, that I was being properly and publicly chastised, the agency removed the Lever accounts from my group. I was humiliated. Within a few weeks, however, I was quietly awarded the American Express Travel account. It's the kind of give-and-take that happens to *Mad Men*'s Peggy Olson all the time.

A lot of marriages didn't survive all of this extracurricular activity. During one brief period while I was at Ogilvy, five of the top men at the agency were deeply involved in extramarital affairs, and left their wives. That accounted for about half of the most senior males at Ogilvy. Three of the five women concerned worked at the agency: one was a secretary, one was a research director, and one worked in the legal department.

The fourth was an actress who appeared in a General Foods commercial. The fifth was a very important client of the agency. Four of these couples ended up getting married, and only one of those marriages didn't work. Not a bad percentage.

The fifth couple didn't have such a happy time of it. Andrew Kershaw was the president of Ogilvy & Mather. He was a Hungarian who escaped to Great Britain during World War II and joined the Commandos. The Brits gave him a new name to avoid possible Nazi reprisals on his parents back in Hungary. Andrew saw a lot of action, most of it parachuting behind enemy lines. He was not an Adonis, but he was dashing, witty, sure of himself, a leader. A number of men who rose to top management at Ogilvy told me Andrew had a lasting impact on their lives.

He had been head of Ogilvy's office in Toronto and did such a good job that D.O. brought him to New York as president. Andrew's wife, Mary, decided to stay in Toronto with the children. As it turned out, that was a big mistake.

Sandra Meyer was head of the Maxwell House coffee brand group at General Foods. Any man at GF would have killed for that job; Sandra was the first woman who ever had it. She was born into the extraordinary Wasserstein family. Her brother, Bruce, was a financial whiz, a head of First Boston. Her sister, Wendy, was a successful playwright, author of the Pulitzer Prize–winning *Heidi Chronicles.* Sandra was not a beauty, but she was charming, witty, sure of herself, a leader. She and Andrew were made for each other.

They had been discreet about the relationship, as was the style at Ogilvy. One evening, I was waiting for Michael in the Grill Room at the Four Seasons and happened to spot Sandra and Andrew at a nearby table. They didn't see me. In fact, it was pretty obvious that they had eyes only for each other. "Why, they're head over heels in love," I said to myself.

Soon after that, the affair went public. Andrew started divorce proceedings, and he and Sandra lived together quite openly, with Sandra's two daughters. They had a Park Avenue apartment in New York City and a house in the country. It wasn't appropriate for Sandra to continue as an important client of the agency, so she accepted a big job at Citicorp. (In Wendy's play *The Sisters Rosensweig,* the Sandra character is portrayed as a banker, not a packaged-goods marketer.) They planned a wedding. Tom Margittai, partner in the Four Seasons restaurant and by now a good friend of theirs, said that as a wedding present he would give them the best reception ever thrown in New York City.

Andrew never got the divorce. He died suddenly of a heart attack at their country home one bright fall day. There was a lovely, music-filled memorial service. Sandra attended, of course. So did Andrew's wife and children. Jock Elliott, then chairman of Ogilvy, gave one of his most politic speeches. "Andrew had a large and loving family," he said, "all of whom are here today."

The Four Seasons catered the reception afterward at Andrew and Sandra's apartment. None of us there were really very hungry.

It seems to me, looking back on all the marriages breaking up, that it was primarily the most senior men in the agency who were having the serious affairs. Why? First of all, they had the wherewithal that junior guys didn't. They had big private offices with doors that locked. And *couches.* (Junior account men just had chairs.) They had the money to reserve hotel rooms or take off for a weekend.

More important, though, was the fact that these executives gave the agency a higher priority than they gave their marriages; they were devoted to their jobs and worked late four or five nights a week. One man explained it to me this way: "By the time we got home to Connecticut or Westchester or wherever, we were beat, our wives were sleepy, and we didn't have much energy to talk, much less make love. So it was a collision course."

Another man looked back. "There at the office, you had some bright, attractive young woman who was terribly interested in the same things you were, understood what worried you, and was always ready for innovative sex. And there at home was your wife, a little older, a little bored. She didn't understand what you did all day, but as long as you kept climbing the tree and making more money, she would keep playing tennis and bridge and going to the country club. There wasn't much to talk about, and on those rare nights when you might think about sex, she always had a headache."

A former agency head, now in his nineties, told me, with a twinkle in his eye, that he couldn't resist. "I was forty-five years old, and for the first time in my life I was getting blow jobs in the back of a car. I left my wife and married the girl."

Of course, during the summer all the wives would pack up the kids and go off to the Hamptons or Nantucket and leave their husbands alone in the city. *What were they thinking?*

I remember a conversation I had early in my Ogilvy career with Bill Phillips, who was then already in top management, heading for the agency presidency and ultimately its chairmanship. One evening as I was heading home, Bill saw me waiting for the elevator and asked me where I lived. I told him the Upper East Side. "Do you and your husband have dinner together every night?" he asked. "Just about every night," I answered truthfully.

Most of us who worked with Bill knew that his marriage was already rocky. It wasn't standing up to his late nights at the office. "I think having dinner together really helps hold a marriage together," he said, sort of wistfully. I felt sorry for him.

I had only one bad time in all of my years at Ogilvy. I worked for a creative director who continually pressed me to have sex with him. If a man did that today, the woman would simply march into Human Resources and complain of sexual harassment, and the man would be in big trouble. Back then, as I mentioned, that phrase was simply not in our vocabularies. Women who complained were usually ostracized. You were expected to handle things like this without making a big fuss about it.

This man was a creative director like *Mad Men*'s Don Draper; he even looked a little like Don Draper—tall, slim, and attractive. He would ride in on his white horse at the eleventh hour with an idea that saved the account. Everybody adored him; David Ogilvy had personally recruited him and thought the world of him. He taught me to be fearless in writing copy. "Go for the jugular," he'd say. "Don't be afraid to expose yourself." He taught me to look for insights that would hit consumers in the heart or in the guts. He forced me to not settle for little ideas, but to look for big campaigns that could go on for years.

It was hard to complain about this paragon. Anyway, who would I have complained to? There was no "human resources" department at Ogilvy back then. There was an office manager, but he was a man. I certainly couldn't complain to my husband; he would have come to the office with a gun. So, like many women, I endured battering, exhausting, cat-and-mouse harassment that went on for almost two years.

My first inkling of the boss's interest happened when we went to a midwestern city for a meeting with an important new client assigned to our creative group. There were four of us: my creative director, two account management men, and me. I was accustomed to being the only woman in an all-male group, so I felt quite safe. We arrived in the morning, attended meetings all day, had dinner with the client, and were in our hotel rooms by nine P.M. My boss had had quite a lot to drink at dinner but was under control. I was asleep around eleven when I heard someone knocking at my bedroom door. I padded over in my nightshirt and bare feet. "Who is it?" My boss identified himself. "Just a minute," I said. Hotels didn't provide a bathrobe in those days, so I put on my coat, buttoned it, and opened the door.

My boss obviously had enjoyed a few more drinks since we parted after dinner, and now he stood there holding a half-empty scotch bottle. "Is something wrong?" I asked innocently.

"Nothing's wrong. Just thought we'd have a nightcap."

"Just one," I said. "I really need to get to bed."

So we sat there, next to each other on the bed—the only

place two people could sit—drinking warm scotch out of bathroom tumblers. And his hand was on my leg. I need to make clear that I wasn't Little Nell from the country and he wasn't chaining me to the railroad tracks. But he was my *boss*. So I couldn't yell for the house detective. Or slap his face. Or anything much.

"Well, I guess we really need to get to bed." I faked a yawn.

"Yes, we do," he agreed happily, and moved his hand thighward.

"I don't know why it is, but I always seem to need more sleep when I have my period," I said. His hand shot away.

But he didn't give up. Every time we visited that client and had to stay overnight, he'd come knocking on my door. And I'd lie in bed, pretending to be asleep, waiting for him to go away.

When out-of-town seduction didn't work, the creative director began to move on me in the office. One time, we were working on a new product assignment for Lever. He announced that there were too many distractions at the office—telephones ringing, account people appearing in our doorway. We needed a day without interruption. So he had instructed his secretary to book a hotel suite. We would meet there the next morning at nine-thirty. "We really need to come up with the BIG IDEA."

The next morning, precisely at nine-thirty, my boss opened the door of the hotel suite. I stood there with the senior art director. "We really need to come up with the BIG IDEA," I parroted serenely. "So I brought Doug."

Not being able to talk about it to anybody compounded the problem. I began to see a psychiatrist. He didn't understand sexual harassment any more than any other men of the day.

"It's very simple. Just tell him you are happily married and don't want to have an affair."

"But he's my boss."

"So?"

The psychiatrist didn't work. I began to cry in my sleep at night.

The rule of silence (I think the Mafia calls it *omerta)* was absolute. The agency probably honored it more than the Mafia did. But I decided to break the rule and go see David Ogilvy.

I made some lame excuse about wanting to broaden my horizons and work on nonpackaged goods. I stammered that it would be helpful to me to work with a different creative director to learn different advertising styles. Quickly, I ran out of polite fibs and began to cry.

D.O. pretended not to notice. "My dear girl, I think you have every reason to be transferred to another creative group. Let me see what I can do."

In three days, I was assigned to a new group, on a different floor. My old boss and I would see each other perhaps once a year at the annual Ogilvy officers' outing. He would always raise a glass to me from across the room, and I would always toast him back.

I'm sorry it had to end that way. He taught me how to write advertising.

CHAPTER 3

"Get the Money Before They Screw You"

When Shirley Polykoff wrote the famous advertising slogan "Does she . . . or doesn't she?" for Clairol in 1956, only hussies dyed their hair. The slogan took off, and women all over America believed Shirley's reassuring answer to that question: "Hair color so natural, only her hairdresser knows for sure." Within ten years, almost 50 percent of them were coloring their hair (Shirley never used the word "dye"), bringing in about $100 million a year to Clairol, which owned half the market. Her agency, Foote, Cone & Belding, where she had once been the only female copywriter, had a lock on the Clairol business because of her.

She turned millions of women into blondes with campaigns like: "Is it true blondes have more fun?" and "If I've only one life to live, let me live it as a blonde."

I bumped into Shirley at a pro bono advertising event in 1983, about fifteen years before she died. She was already well into her seventies, but her hair was defiantly blond, and coiled in braids on top of her head. She looked like a buxom mother figure from *Fiddler on the Roof,* good Russian-Jewish peasant stock—which is exactly what she was.

She waggled a finger at me, inviting me to join her in a corner of the booth she was manning. "I've always liked you, Jane, and you're becoming a great success. So I want to give you this piece of advice. It could make a big difference to you." I said I was all ears.

"Get the money before they screw you, darling," she said. "Before they screw you the way they screwed me."

The official Foote, Cone story is that they doubled Shirley's salary twice in the early days. But women copywriters were earning just pittances. Most women who were writers in the fifties and sixties recall that they were making between thirty-five and fifty dollars a week, about half the salary of a male copywriter. On *Mad Men,* when Peggy Olson is promoted from secretary to part-time copywriter, she asks for a raise from thirty-five dollars a week to forty. "That's fifteen percent," warns her boss, the creative director. Account man Pete Campbell explains to his bride why they can't afford to buy an apartment. "I'm only making seventy-five dollars a week," he says, but adds that he'll soon be making a lot more. Shirley could indeed have had her salary doubled and she still wouldn't have been making what a man earned.

Advertising was considered a glamorous field by scores of young women advancing on New York like lemmings, leaping from their secure ivy-covered heights into the world of Madison Avenue, completely unaware of what went on inside an agency. They soon discovered they could become either typists or secretaries, depending on whether they had shorthand. Shelly Lazarus, chairman of Ogilvy & Mather, is considered one of the most powerful women in American business today. After graduating from Smith College, she wanted to work in advertising, but was offered only secretarial jobs. "I didn't type that well and it didn't sound that interesting to me. A woman who worked at one of the agencies suggested that I get an MBA. She said, 'I think if you have an MBA, they can't make you type.' "

Several agencies created what they called "junior copywriter groups." Linda Bird Francke worked in such a group at Young & Rubicam when she was hired, fresh out of college, in 1959. "Junior copywriter, hell," she says. "It was a typing pool. None of us could really type; we'd been English majors or art history majors. And now all we did all day was type radio scripts and storyboards. There were no Xerox machines, so if you needed to make a lot of copies of anything, the only way to do it was to mimeograph. You typed a stencil—it took about a hundred pounds of pressure for every stroke—and then somebody from the mailroom ran it through." Linda was one of the rare ones who actually was promoted to writing copy. After working for me at Ogilvy, she left advertising to become an award-winning journalist and author. She wrote or collaborated on a dozen books, among them bestselling biographies of Betty Friedan and Barbara Walters.

Marikay Hartigan started as a "copy typist" at Ogilvy in the late fifties. She was making fifty dollars a week. "I was twenty-three years old, an Irish Catholic kid from Chicago, and I didn't know anything. In addition to typing print ads and radio scripts and storyboards, I answered the telephone for all eight people in the creative department. David Ogilvy was always looking for his copywriters; they were never there, and I never knew where they were. So he would bang down the phone in disgust. One day he called, looking for his own secretary. As usual, I told him I didn't know. 'She's probably at Rattazzi's,' he said, 'fornicating with copywriters.' "

Marikay wanted to be a copywriter and kept pestering the agency's copy chief to give her a creative assignment. Finally she was allowed to try her hand at a radio script for Pepperidge Farm. "It was presented to the client, so I was ecstatic. Naturally, I didn't get invited to the meeting, but I was ecstatic anyway."

She was a good copywriter, and soon she was getting more assignments from the copy chief for Pepperidge Farm and Dove soap. Like Peggy Olson, Marikay continued her clerical duties for about a year, writing the ads at night and on weekends. Finally, she was promoted to copywriter and given a ten-dollar raise.

Marikay left Ogilvy four years later because she was going to marry a fellow copywriter at the agency, Joel Raphaelson, and David Ogilvy had that rule against nepotism. "What would you do if Joel and I just decided to live together?" she asked David. "We don't have any guidelines about living in sin," he answered. "I never asked for a raise," Marikay told me. "It never occurred to me. They gave me a ten-dollar raise every year, so by the time I left, I was making ninety dollars a week. I thought that was a lot."

Ask any woman who worked at an advertising agency in the *Mad Men* era. Of course we didn't make the same salary as a man with the same title, even if we knew we were doing a better job. We didn't even have equal *space*—the guys got offices with windows; we got cubicles. The problem was that we simply submitted to the situation. Women's lib had not yet flowered, and our consciousnesses had definitely not been raised.

Why should men take us seriously as advertising professionals? Women weren't even taken seriously as *consumers*. We were at best decorative fluff heads; our biggest concerns were ring around the collar and wax buildup on the kitchen floor. David Ogilvy wrote his famous statement "The consumer is not a moron; she is your wife," but the stereotypes persisted. Futurist Laurel Cutler, one of only seven living women in the Advertising Hall of Fame, recalls that the agency she worked for handled U.S. Rubber, the tire maker. "Without bothering to talk to me or to any other women, they came up with the idea for a tire for women. This was not a white-walled tire. It was a *pink-walled* tire. A *pink-walled tire.*"

Why would anyone ask women what they thought about products? David Ogilvy was a rare exception. He respected research and he respected consumers, even if they happened to be women. He had worked for the Gallup research organization, where he polled a lot of women, and he knew they often provided insights about products that led to persuasive advertising. (In one of his books, *Ogilvy on Advertising,* he devotes an entire chapter to the subject. It is titled "18 Miracles of Research.") Ogilvy & Mather was one of the first agencies to establish an entire department devoted to research. Over at J. Walter Thompson, Rena Bartos was just starting to form a research department. "It turned out to be a mostly female department," Rena says. "I didn't set about to hire women, but you got more for your money. I could hire a woman Ph.D. for eighteen thousand dollars [a year]."

Ten years later, Jerry Della Femina was recruiting talented staffers for his own young agency, and he hired lots of women. "We developed a reputation for being very pro-feminist, very liberated," Jerry recalls, "but that wasn't the reason at all. If a man was asking for a hundred thousand dollars, you could hire a woman for sixty thousand. He was only worth sixty thousand dollars and she was worth eighty thousand dollars. That was a big swing."

Shelly Lazarus tells about discussions on women's products, like tampons, held in rooms filled with men from the client side and the agency side. "There would invariably come that moment when these men were arguing about which was the right approach and then someone would turn to me and ask, 'Well, Shelly, what do *women* think?' So I actually wielded this enormous power because I was speaking on behalf of all women in the country. And whatever I said was believed. Because I was the only woman present. And how did the men know?"

If we couldn't balance our checkbooks, men figured, why should they pay us the same salaries as men? Would we notice? Would we care? To a large extent, they were right. We had no negotiating skills and were uncomfortable asking for money; it felt kind of whorish. In some weird way, it almost seemed proper for a man to earn more. A woman copywriter at Ogilvy discovered she was making a lot less than a colleague. She complained to her boss, who reacted with surprise. "But he's a *man* with a wife and kids to support." "I accepted that explanation as totally plausible," she said, "and I didn't ask again." A male copywriter at Ogilvy in the same era told his boss he was getting married, and immediately received a raise of several thousand dollars. "This will help with the mortgage," he was told. No woman in all my interviews told me she was rewarded for getting married. It usually went the other way.

Creative director and novelist Anne Tolstoi Wallach applied for a writer's job at *Time* magazine in the late 1950s. She was told that only men were writers; women worked as researchers. "I didn't feel that was discriminatory at all. That was the way things were." She decided to go into advertising instead.

My first job in New York City, after Bucknell and a Fulbright and a master's degree in English from Cornell, was a secretarial job at Time Inc. (Actually, I wanted to be an actress. I spent most of my time at Bucknell on the stage, but at this point I needed some income to support myself while I went on auditions.) I had taught myself to type at Cornell, in order to save money by typing my own thesis, and I learned to take dictation not by using any shorthand, but by writing like the wind and having an excellent memory.

Like Anne Wallach, I completely accepted the fact that no women could rise to be writers at the magazine. I decided to become a researcher, but I never got the chance to try to break into their ranks. One evening I was walking down Broadway with two unemployed actor friends who were lamenting that all they needed was one break. A woman stopped us and asked *me* if I would like to be a contestant on the quiz show *Name That Tune*. Obviously, I looked like the kind of person who would jump up and down, squeal with delight, and kiss the master of ceremonies. Of course I said yes. So I went on the show, and I won $150—which was a fortune to me then, more than two weeks' pay. More important, the producer, Harry Salter, spotted some creative spark in me and hired me to interview the contestants. I loved working in television. At least temporarily, I was back in show business.

And I was very good at my job. What set *Name That Tune* apart from other quiz shows was the fact that two contestants worked in partnership, over a period of five weeks or more, to win the big $25,000 prize. I pulled out everything I had learned about literature and the theater to suggest new ideas for these couplings. How about teaming up an Irish-American guy with an Israeli woman? And, wait a minute, maybe she is an officer in the Israeli army. Oh, and as she is about to leave to go home to Tel Aviv, we'll have the man's father, who has a sort of Barry Fitzgerald brogue, give her a shamrock to plant in the Holy Land. And we'll have him come right up and be on camera and say that old Irish prayer: "May the road rise to meet you, may the wind be always at your back, and may the good Lord hold you in the palm of his hand."

I would listen hard to the way people talked, and fit their own speech into the conversation with the emcee. For a laconic cowboy, I suggested the following dialogue. Emcee: "Benny, I see that you are from Helena, Montana." Benny: "Yep." Emcee: "And you are a cowboy?" Benny: "Yep." Emcee: "The kind who rides in rodeos?" Benny: "Yep." Emcee: "Benny, do you always talk this much?" Benny: "Nope."

The husband-to-be of a contestant from Kansas, a hardworking farmer named Reuben, talked in almost biblical aphorisms. So, on the show just before the wedding, we called him up on stage, and the emcee asked his views about marriage. Reuben said simply, "Marriage is sort of like a farm. The more love you give it, the better the harvest you reap." The audience in the studio burst into applause. So did I. I wrote the lines, I rehearsed Reuben, and he delivered them perfectly.

Harry Salter liked my ideas. He would send forth his little army of contestant scouts, and they would return with real people who might have stepped out of central casting, they were so perfect. It turned out that the American audience liked my ideas, too. The show's ratings soared. Mr. Salter (I called him *Mister* Salter until the day he died) made me associate producer, and gave me a raise to one hundred and fifty dollars a week—a lofty title and salary for a twenty-five-year-old woman in 1957.

The world of television in the 1960s was a man's world, just like the world of business. In television, women were lowly production assistants; we sometimes rose to be assistant producers, but that title really meant glorified clerk-typist-gofer. In the world of advertising, women could be copywriters, but we were relegated to "female" accounts like food, fashion, and cosmetics. We were not regarded as threats until we began to invade traditional men's enclaves like the automotive accounts. At that point, the men began to circle the wagons. When Anne Wallach was promoted into the Ford creative group at J. Walter Thompson, the men's reception was actually hostile. "They didn't want me at meetings, they didn't want me at shoots, they simply didn't want me. The basic assumption was that if you had a husband who was any good, you wouldn't be there."

Hiring women in the creative area was one thing. Making them *account executives* was even more challenging to the establishment. It's curious to me that several men now vie for the honor of being first to hire a female account executive at Ogilvy. Ken Roman told me proudly that he was the pioneer. "Gillette had given us some cosmetics business, and I was tired of going home every night and having to ask my wife what was the difference between eyeliner and eye shadow. She suggested I hire a woman." It was a revolutionary idea: a woman account person working on products sold to women. The young woman he hired was a Harvard Business School graduate. She did brilliantly, the account prospered, and Roman decided she deserved a raise. He went to his boss for approval. The boss looked at the salary history. "Why does she need a raise? She's making a lot of money for a *girl*."

Another top Ogilvy executive, John Blaney, told me proudly that *he* was the first to tap a woman for account management. With the approval of her boss, he promoted a secretary to the position of assistant account executive. The truth seems to be that Roman was the first to hire a woman MBA from the outside, while Blaney was the first to promote a woman from the secretarial arena. I began to see a pattern in my interviews with men: every one of them bragged about his trailblazing promotion of women. One man even had the courage to reveal that a woman he hired rose to outrank him and, eventually, fired him.

In any event, these hirings were the opening salvo in a competition that heated up in the 1970s. Women who had worked their way up through the ranks from clerical work into account management faced women arriving with business school credentials. Ultimately, the women with business school training won the day. I suppose the outcome was predictable. The MBAs had weaponry not part of a woman's traditional arsenal. They could talk about profit and loss, return on investment, and gross rating points. Just as important, many of them were working for men who didn't have business degrees and were dazzled by their knowledge.

I was hired as a copywriter at Ogilvy in 1964 at ten thousand dollars and left in 1976 making forty thousand. The chairman of the agency told me as I was leaving that it was the most meteoric pay hike he had ever seen. Yet my salary barely budged for the first few years. I caught up due to a fluke.

I had been reading some psychological studies about the importance of the sense of smell as an indicator of product performance ("Maxwell House coffee tastes as good as it smells," was one advertising tagline). This led our creative team to suggest an idea to Lever Brothers for Dove dishwashing liquid. Since it was positioned as gentle to hands and contained a hand lotion ingredient, why didn't Lever change its scent to almond, just like Jergens lotion? To call attention to the new formula, we suggested they hang a collar around every bottle that said: PICK ME UP AND SMELL ME. Our clients loved the idea, and rushed the new product, complete with neck hangers, into a few test markets.

One of the test areas was Tenafly, New Jersey, right across the George Washington Bridge. Gene Grayson sent me over to spend a day in a supermarket interviewing women in the dish soap aisle. I pushed a shopping cart while a photographer with a handheld 16 mm camera hid nearby. Anytime a woman picked up a Dove bottle, I would pounce, pretending to be a dim-witted housewife, and ask what it smelled like. Many of them said it smelled like a hand lotion; a few even volunteered that it *worked* like a hand lotion and protected your hands while you did the dishes.

We had intended these interviews purely as an internal presentation to our clients. The Lever folks loved the footage so much, they decided we had to edit it into a thirty-second commercial for the national television campaign. Of course, there was no way to cut me out of the footage. David Ogilvy had to give special permission, because one of his rules prohibited agency employees from appearing in our own commercials. (Remember Angelique, the other exception.) I ended up earning residuals from the American Federation of Television and Radio Artists, and made about two thousand dollars over the six months the commercial ran. "That amounts to a nice raise for you," Gene said. "And just about what I was going to give you. Funny, the way things happen." So, that year, Gene didn't give me a raise. The next year, I reminded him of the raise he'd planned to give me, and he realized it was an unheard-of 20 percent hike. He was a man of his word, though, and even if it made him grit his teeth, he got me the money. Funny, the way things happen.

In my early days as a copywriter, there were no women writing anywhere in the agency on "male" accounts like cars, alcoholic beverages, or finance. I was the first woman to be assigned to the American Express account. The two Ogilvy account men, escorting me downtown to the American Express building for my first meeting, were understandably nervous. "Don't be surprised if the guys don't seem very friendly," one warned me. "They're concerned they'll have to watch their language around you." The second account executive added, "And they're afraid if they ever turn down creative work, you'll cry." I began to feel nervous myself.

As they predicted, the young American Express clients were a little on the chilly side, but not downright hostile. We stood around the conference table, shifting from foot to foot. I didn't want to be the first to sit down; neither did anyone else. Then an older man entered the room, and all the guys sprang to attention. I didn't know who he was, but someone had the presence of mind to introduce us. Howard Clark was the highest of the high, the client of clients, the CEO of American Express. He shook my hand warmly, escorted me to the table, and pulled out a chair. *This isn't going to be so bad,* I thought. "Did you forget your steno pad, dear?" he asked. "We can get you one."

"We didn't expect you at this meeting, Mr. Clark," one of his staff said. Clark smiled jovially. "I heard that a hotshot new copywriter from Ogilvy has just been assigned to our business," he said. "Which one is he?"

Only a few women were brave enough to start their own agencies. Olivia Trager and Marcella Rosen set up shop, and their first new business presentation was to a hotel chain. The potential client asked them what their fee structure was and Marcella told him. "We don't pay hookers that much," he said.

Pat Martin and Joan Lipton went into business about the same time as the Martin & Lipton Agency. "It wasn't very big, but we managed," Lipton recalls. "We worked on a lot of accounts men didn't want anything to do with, like baby food and diapers."

The turning point for women in advertising came in 1966

when the legendary Mary Wells opened Wells Rich Greene with the Braniff airline account. She convinced Braniff to paint the fleet every color of the rainbow and announced the fact with a two-page magazine spread announcing "The End of the Plain Plane." She convinced them to hire Emilio Pucci to design uniforms for the stewardesses, and rechristened them "hostesses." Pucci conceived sexy outfits that they could take off, one layer at a time, as the plane flew to warm destinations. Finally they got down to harem pajamas. The agency announced this news in a commercial called "The Air Strip," shocking for its day.

Everything Mary did made news. It was a big story when she and Harding Lawrence, head of Braniff, married in 1967. He was running an airline and she was running an agency. In her candid autobiography, *A Big Life in Advertising,* Mary writes that it never entered her mind that she would leave the agency or that she and Harding would have "a traditional marriage living and working in the same town." So Harding lived in Dallas, and Mary lived in New York. Every Friday she flew to Texas and spent the weekend being a wife to Harding and a mother to their two daughters. Then every Sunday she flew back. It must have been exhausting.

I went to work for Wells Rich Greene in 1976. They promised me a senior vice presidency, twenty thousand dollars more a year than I'd been making, and the chance to work on Procter & Gamble accounts. It was too dazzling to refuse. The reason for this seductive offer was the just-published *How to Advertise,* which I co-authored with Ken Roman. (The title had been given to us by David Ogilvy, who loathed every one of the hundreds of titles we suggested. His suggestion worked;

Jane's official photo her first day at Wells Rich Greene, 1976.

the book is still in print thirty-six years later.) *How to Advertise* was full of advice on "positioning" and "strategy" and creative work that paid off the "promise" or "key consumer benefit." WRG had recently been scolded by P&G, a prize client, because its creative teams were not following the strategic direction closely enough. So president and creative director Charlie Moss reached out to me.

By then, both Rich and Greene had departed wealthy men, and Mary was very much in charge. In addition to P&G, our accounts included TWA (which had replaced Braniff), Bic, Alka-Seltzer, Benson & Hedges cigarettes, Midas mufflers, and, soon to arrive, the state of New York, my own particular baby. We occupied three entire floors of the block-square General Motors Building, extravagant space with views out over Central Park. I remember polished wood floors with Persian rugs, offices with original artwork on the walls instead of prints, and a grand staircase between two of the floors.

One day when Mary wasn't there, someone showed Shelly Lazarus around her office. In the middle of the room was one of those rolling racks used at department stores, with dozens of outfits covered in plastic. Shelly was entranced. "It turned out that Mary had a personal shopper at Bergdorf, and when the shopper found something she thought Mary would like, she'd send it over. So it would be there when Mary returned and she could decide whether she wanted it or not. To me this was the most fabulous, sophisticated existence that I could even imagine."

I suspect Mary had personal shoppers because she didn't have time to shop herself. She worked twelve-, thirteen-, fourteen-hour days, but she never looked tired. She never allowed herself to look tired. It was one part the theatrical training of her early years and a kind of "show must go on" tradition, one part iron discipline, and one part an inner spiritual self that few people recognized in Mary. She also had an almost supernatural ability to ferret out her clients' problems. At a meeting, I would watch her say to a P&G brand manager, "I'm sure you're worried about the test market in Indianapolis, but I have an idea about how to fix it." The man's eyes would go wide with shock, because that test market was a big secret and yes, he was worried about it because the new product was tanking. And the next minute, his eyes would grow even wider in reverence. Mary knew about the test market, God knows why, and Mary could fix it, God knows how. And maybe he'd keep his job; maybe he'd even be promoted. Because of Mary. And he'd join the line of worshippers filing up the nave.

Everybody at WRG belonged to the cult of Mary, and I was no exception. I worshipped her, was in awe of her, and was a bit afraid of her at the same time. She was always elegant, perfectly dressed, coiffed, and made up. Despite endless client lunches and dinners, she never gained an ounce. Mary had lunch served to all her senior officers every day; it was one of our most prized perks. Every day, week in and week out, Mary ate a lunch of raw vegetables, elegantly served on imported china, accompanied by water in a crystal glass. At dinner with clients she drank water on the rocks in a cocktail glass until everyone had finished their first two drinks. Only then would Mary sometimes allow herself a real martini. She confided to me once that she was always grateful when she didn't have to entertain anyone at dinner; she would come home from the office, immediately get into bed, and have her meal served on a tray. She thought that was heavenly. I did too.

Yet she seemed tireless. I remember rehearsing one night for an important new business pitch. There were twenty-five or thirty of us taking part: copywriters, art directors, strategists, research directors. As we went over every step of our presentation for the following morning, Mary made detailed comments on everything from the content to the style: use a bolder verb here; insert the name of the client there; speak in a softer voice at the beginning, louder at the end. By the time we finished, it was after eleven and everybody was exhausted. Mary stood up and smiled at us. "Now," she said, "let's do it again, and this time let's get it right."

When I interviewed Mary for this book, I asked how she attained her extraordinary self-discipline. Her reply seems to me important career advice for women today.

"Early on I learned to focus and eliminate from my life anything that didn't really matter because so much in my life *did* matter. I pretty well eliminated a social life except with my clients. They were as interesting to socialize with as anyone else I knew, so that was easy. My life was very simply my family, Wells Rich Greene, and my clients. My husband traveled around the world for his work. We met in interesting places when we could. We took the children with us when they weren't in school.

"My mother used to tuck me in bed nights, always saying: 'You can have everything you want in life if you are willing to work hard enough for it,' and I believed her. So I was never sucking my thumb wishing anything was at all different."

Mary always had time to be thoughtful and gracious, to

clients and to the folks at the agency. Once she sent me a single sprig of lily of the valley in a tiny vase. Her note said: "This reminds me of you. Small and special." Other gifts followed over the years, always selected personally by Mary, and always with a handwritten note.

She invited me to her apartment one day for a baby shower she was hosting for an assistant. I was going to sit on the couch, but it was so pristine, so untouched—its pillows so perfectly plumped—that I sat in a chair instead. That couch made me realize suddenly: *This apartment isn't really lived in*. I looked over at Mary and thought for the first time that she might be lonely by herself in New York.

The agency name remained *Wells* Rich Greene, but Mary was definitely Mrs. Harding Lawrence. She introduced herself as Mary Lawrence. Her secretary answered the telephone "Mrs. Lawrence's office." In her autobiography, Mary writes that from the moment they met, she and Harding had an "infinite connection" that would never change.

Harding Lawrence died in January 2002. Mary and I exchanged notes. My husband, Michael, died just three months later. Mary, the most famous, most successful, and highest-paid woman in the history of advertising, wrote to me then. "Let's get together and try to figure out what we are going to do with the rest of our lives."

I believe Mary has indeed figured it out. Her note to me in early 2011 said: "I have loved living my life. I love living it now."

I hope you are happy, Mary. You deserve to be.

CHAPTER 4

Women and Children Last

The term "working mother" was an oxymoron in the 1960s. It was almost unheard of for the mother of children under ten or twelve to work full-time unless the family badly needed the income. Men felt vaguely sorry for working mothers; we must be married to real deadbeats. Women, especially other mothers, were usually shocked to learn we were letting other people raise our children. The term "stay-at-home mom" had not yet been invented; there was no need for it. That's what moms did; they stayed home.

Lee Aiges was one of the first women at Ogilvy to be promoted from secretarial to account work. In 1967 she was a mom at home with two little kids in Fort Lee, New Jersey. She remembers saying: "I can't do this anymore. I'll do anything. I'll sweep floors. But I'm getting a job." Her mother, hearing this decision, asked: "You're *what*? What will people say?"

Laurel Cutler, already a mother of three and a full-time copywriter at McCann-Erickson, moved with her husband and young children to South Orange, New Jersey, in the late

1950s. She went to a meeting of the Wellesley Club to get to know some neighbors. They wanted to know where she lived, what her husband did, and how many children she had. When they discovered Laurel worked full-time the first question they asked, somewhat accusingly, was "What do you do when the children are sick?"

I was a full-time working mother in September 1965 when I took my daughter Kate to her first day of first grade at the Nightingale-Bamford School. The mothers of new girls were all asked to hang around the school until noon every day for two weeks or so, to reassure the children. I left at nine fifteen every day to go to work. The other mothers and the school administration both regarded me with suspicion that lasted for years.

Helen Bishop, the only full-time working mother on *Mad Men* (at least in the first four seasons) is ostracized by the other mothers. She is divorced, doesn't keep an immaculate house, and feeds her children frozen foods. Betty Draper fills in for a sick babysitter one night so Helen can stuff envelopes for Kennedy mailings. She snoops inside the medicine cabinet and finds the unmistakable clamshell shape of a diaphragm container. Betty's expression tells us this confirms her suspicions that Helen sleeps around.

Most colleges—especially women's colleges—subtly underscored the notion that a woman's destiny was to marry and have children. The male president of all-female Radcliffe is said to have told freshmen in the 1950s that their four years would prepare them to be splendid wives and mothers, and the reward might be to marry Harvard men. The male president of another women's college declared that the curriculum should include cooking.

Shelly Lazarus tells of the traditional hoop rolling performed by the seniors on graduation day at Smith. "The quad wasn't large enough to hold us all at one time, so we were divided into two heats. Engaged girls went first; non-engaged girls went second. There was no question as to which group was preferred."

Another Smith alumna, Betty Friedan, who graduated in 1942, went back in 1959 to spend a week on campus interviewing the students. She was preparing to write an article that would morph into her groundbreaking book, *The Feminine Mystique.* Friedan asked one senior what courses the women were excited about that year. The young woman looked at her as though she were "some prehistoric dinosaur" and said, "Girls don't get excited about things like that anymore. . . . Everybody wants to graduate with a diamond ring on her finger."

When I was at Bucknell University in the early fifties, women were definitely "the second sex." Freshman women had to be in our dorms by eight o'clock every night. There were no exceptions, not even to go to the library. After freshman year, we were allowed to stay out until eleven. And one night annually, the night of the senior prom, we received special "late permissions" until midnight.

Our dormitories were segregated, located in a separate campus fortress at the bottom of the hill. It was known as "the Sem," a holdover from the days when those buildings housed the nineteenth-century Women's Seminary. Bucknell coeds were still called "Sem Gems." There was a housemother—sometimes two—in every dorm. Men were not allowed above the ground-floor lobbies. Every once in a while, a father would penetrate the barrier; a shout would go up of "man on third" or whatever the floor was, and girls in various stages of undress would run for cover.

We were allowed to entertain gentleman callers in just one area, Hunt Hall living room, a vast, chilly, formal Victorian cavern of a place. There, the "three feet on the floor" rule was strictly enforced. Out of any respective couple's four feet, three had to be firmly planted on the floor at all times. The housemothers went around and checked.

Jane and fellow Bucknellian Philip Roth star in the 1952 university production of Jean Giraudoux's *The Madwoman of Chaillot.*

The most exciting moments happened at the women's dining hall almost every week, when a table would begin singing "Best Wishes to You" (to the tune of "Happy Birthday") and we would all join in, craning our necks to see who was the lucky girl who'd gotten "pinned" the night before. Wearing your boyfriend's fraternity pin was almost as good as being engaged, a step that usually followed. In many ways it was better, because his whole fraternity would gather beneath the girl's window one night a week or so after the pinning and serenade her with fraternity songs about "the girl of my dreams" and eternal love and such. I ached to be pinned, but I never was. Michael did give me his Delta Kappa Epsilon pin, but that was after we were married. So it wasn't the same; there was no serenade.

Bucknell tried hard to prepare us to be good little suburban housewives like *Mad Men*'s Betty Draper. On Sunday, we always had "Sunday dinner" at noon instead of lunch. You knew it was a special meal because the turkey—and it was always turkey—was accompanied by a little ball of lemon sherbet in a tiny white paper cup. After the meal, we were all asked to gather in the aforementioned Hunt Hall living room. There, in our Sunday-best outfits and panty girdles and nylons with seams and high heels, we would receive an etiquette lesson in the proper way to pour tea or coffee from silver servers.

Women at Bucknell were never without chaperones. At fraternity parties, there were always the obligatory two faculty couples who played bridge in a room apart and discreetly averted their eyes from any questionable activity. The fraternities were allowed to invite the chaperones of their choice, so younger faculty members, liberal in their views, were in great demand. Bucknell was in a dry county, so liquor was forbidden, but most fraternities served it anyway, usually somewhere in the basement. Coeds often got tipsy, and then we had to protect each other from being reported to housemothers. My junior-year roommate drank martinis all evening at a fraternity bash and had to climb three flights up the fire escape to sneak into our dorm, two hours after curfew. She told me she had fallen asleep in her boyfriend's room. I never questioned her. Most of the coeds followed a sort of "Don't ask, don't tell" rule. You never really knew if your best friend was "saving herself" for the marriage bed and might stigmatize you for engaging in premarital hanky-panky. Or vice versa.

The wildest party on campus was "the Sammy Sand Blast," hosted by Sigma Alpha Mu, the "Jewish fraternity," known as "Sammys." It was a clever way to induce Bucknell women to show as much flesh as was legally possible. Every year in mid-February, the Sammys would remove all the furniture from the ground floor of their house, truck in several tons of sand, and set up beach blankets and umbrellas. The girls who attended all wore the two-piece bathing suits then in fashion, revealing a seductive patch of midriff. Bikinis were worn by fashion models at that point, but not by nice girls. All that sand was a problem, though. Philip Roth, briefly a Sammy at Bucknell, told me that after the party there was sand in the food for months. It was one of the reasons he deactivated.

There were panty raids, of course, about once a year, in spring. Every college had to have one. The men would all gather outside the women's dorms. Some of the more daring fellows would climb up the fire escapes; some of the bolder girls would drop panties out of the windows. The girls always shrieked in mock terror and egged the boys on. Then, just like clockwork, the dean of women would appear and call the dean of men, who would arrive with the campus police, and the "riot" would be over. Everyone knew their lines, the performance always went on as scheduled, and it was all very civilized.

Bucknell also tried to teach us women that sexual activity needed guidelines. We operated under an honor system (the men did not) with an honor council. Any girl who broke any rule was hauled before the honor council and (usually) punished. I discovered in my senior year that there was a guideline about "appropriate kissing" (brief and decorous) and "inappropriate kissing" (prolonged and passionate). I was charged with committing the inappropriate kind, and was sentenced to be in my dorm by eight P.M. for three nights of a spring weekend. I was humiliated and angry, as well as outraged at having to miss two nights of play rehearsals. How dare they put *me,* Janie Brown—president of the drama society, editor of the yearbook, junior year Phi Beta Kappa—under house arrest? Worst of all, I was in the midst of my first and only campus romance. He was an actor, not a fraternity man; Jewish, from Brooklyn. What stung the most was my suspicion that my sorority sisters might have turned me in to the honor council in order to reprimand me not for inappropriate kissing, but for inappropriate mate selection.

I didn't get caught in my most flagrant violation of the honor system in my entire four years. It was a Saturday night in late fall of my freshman year, and the sororities were all having elaborate ceremonies welcoming the new members. We Kappa Delta pledges were asked to wear white dresses as symbols of our innocence, like novices entering a religious order. At the end of the proceedings the sisters presented us each with a white rose and sang a song about our all being just as pure and spotless as the flower.

Most of the girls then went off together to the Bison, our campus coffee shop, but I stole off alone to go downtown to meet a man in his apartment! This was an act so unsanctioned, so impossible, that it was not even specifically forbidden in the honor handbook. I was stagestruck. Bill, a junior at Bucknell, was considered the best actor in the campus drama society. He was the leading man in the upcoming Cap & Dagger play and had invited me to help him rehearse his lines. As befitted a true bohemian, Bill was not living in a dorm, but had an apartment in town. I knew the risk I was taking, but I would have walked through fire.

Bill opened his door and there I was, in my white dress, clutching my white rose. “I didn’t think you’d do it,” he said approvingly. I, in my new role as woman of the world, simply shrugged knowingly. We rehearsed his lines for almost an hour, and then Bill said I could also help him rehearse for the big love scene. After a few kisses, he announced portentously, “Look what I have for you!” It was the tone of voice a man might use to say he was about to bestow on you a diamond, a Mercedes-Benz, a castle in Spain. What Bill had for me was a penis. I had never seen one before, and I fled. I was back in my dorm before I realized I’d forgotten my white rose.

After college, women who did not manage to marry immediately sighed, shrugged their shoulders, and went to work. They knew, as did everybody, that they would continue working only until they were married, or at most until they were pregnant. At that point, your working days were over. In an advertising agency of the 1960s, a baby shower sounded the death knell of your career.

Men thought it was bad enough that they had to put up with women other than secretaries, but at least with a single woman the guys could make passes all day long without feeling guilty. As soon as a woman got married, she became a time bomb: a potentially *pregnant* woman. No agencies wanted large-bellied women hanging about. They set a bad example for other women, and they were terribly upsetting to the men who worked with them. A man couldn't criticize them; their hormones were all unbalanced now, so they might cry. A man couldn't ask them to bring him coffee or pour a drink or lift an ashtray; they might give birth right there in the office. So the best thing to do was get rid of them as quickly as possible. And not invite them back.

Anne Wallach told me she was at Ogilvy from 1951 to 1952, "pregnant most of the time and giving David Ogilvy fits because of it." Quite obviously pregnant, she was heading into a conference room for a client meeting when David intercepted her. "He ordered me not to attend. When I asked him why, he said I would be too distressing to the clients. I think maybe I was distressing to him."

It took twenty years before David accepted pregnant women in the office, but the whole process still made him uncomfortable. Shelly Lazarus remembers being heavily into her ninth month and in her office one evening at about six o'clock, when she looked up to find D.O. standing in her doorway. " 'Are you all right?' he asked. Clearly, he had never seen a woman nine months pregnant in an office before. He came in every day for the rest of my pregnancy and always asked the same question: 'Are you all right?' "

Most agencies had firm policies about pregnancy: women were asked to leave at four or five months, just about the time when they would start to "show" and make men nervous. There was no maternity leave, paid or unpaid. When you left to have a baby, you definitely *left.* A woman who worked at Young & Rubicam, where the cutoff was five months, bragged to me that she had evaded discovery until her seventh month. "I didn't look very pregnant until then." Another woman said she managed to work throughout her entire pregnancy by wearing enormous muumuus. "Most people at the agency thought I'd gotten a little weird and become a hippie, but that was acceptable. Being pregnant was not."

Those few women who wanted to keep working after their babies were born had still another hurdle: taking as little time as possible for the whole birthing process. I was still working in television when both our daughters were born, and show business was tolerant about pregnancies. However, the show must go on, so when Kate was born in 1959, I took just a week off. Four years later, when Jenny arrived, Mabel met me at New York Hospital two days later. She took the baby home. I got into a taxi and went to work.

One of the biggest problems faced by working mothers was child care. Our employers didn't help. Neither did the schools. There were no day-care centers. There were no after-school programs. There were certainly no nurseries in corporations or advertising agencies. And the last thing any of us ever wanted to do was bring our kids to the office if there was a babysitting crisis. We all pretended that we had everything under control

100 percent of the time. We were cool, serene, crisply professional. Having a noisy, dirty, crying child right under everybody's noses would ruin that image.

When Kate started first grade, in a class of eighteen little girls, there were only two full-time working mothers. The other mom and I discovered each other as we sneaked furtively away shortly after nine instead of staying around as the school requested. We walked to the Fifth Avenue bus and wondered whether our daughters would suffer from this in later life.

Eight years later, when Kate entered Nightingale's high school, the headmistress held a meeting of all freshman parents. She warned us of the dangers threatening our daughters, including sex, alcohol, pot, and common everyday girlish gatherings that would interfere with homework. She urgently requested that all the mothers—the *mothers,* not the fathers—be at home every day when the girls returned from school so we could monitor their behavior. Most of the mothers, still not working, meekly agreed. I said I could not possibly be home by three P.M. every day, but added that my housekeeper, the renowned Mabel, was a more formidable chaperone than I could ever be. The headmistress regarded me with familiar suspicion. Wasn't I the same one who wouldn't stay at school with my first grader?

It wasn't until Jenny started high school in 1977 that Nightingale-Bamford began to have its consciousness raised. In a meeting of freshman parents *that* year, the same headmistress told us that our daughters needed to get the best possible education. She predicted that according to the statistics of the day, 50 percent of them would end up divorced, and they would need to make money to support themselves. By this time there were three or four of us working mothers in the group, and we all applauded. The other mothers looked shocked. The fathers looked even more shocked.

There weren't many working mothers at Ogilvy & Mather. Elaine Reiss, the agency's first full-time lawyer, cleverly managed to give birth to her second child over the long Thanksgiving weekend, and came right back to work. When I saw her in her office the following week, I knew we were kindred souls. She and I always greeted each other in the hallway with "Hi, working mother." The president of the agency heard this exchange one day and asked, "What about working fathers? Don't we deserve some respect?" We pooh-poohed him. Working fathers didn't have to shop and cook dinner; they were married to stay-at-home moms.

"They didn't cut us any slack for motherhood," says Linda Bird Francke, who was the rarest bird of all, a *single* working mom. She and I both remember the time when David Ogilvy went on one of his annual crusades about punctuality, particularly in the creative department. His copy chief duly appointed himself monitor of arrival times and secretly ordered all the receptionists to write down the exact minute that creative people came to work. A week after this practice began, Linda and I both received notes warning us that we were consistently tardy. "Late every single day!" our notes read. We pleaded the same case; we had young children to drop off at school, the doors didn't open until eight-thirty, and we couldn't leave our children, at their age, standing alone on the sidewalk. Our explanations fell on deaf ears. The weekly scolding notes continued until the punctuality campaign went away.

All of us working mothers knew the unspoken rules of the

road. You never confessed to taking time off because of a sick child; instead, you explained that *you* had a touch of the flu. It was perfectly acceptable to leave the office for an hour to see your shrink, but not to go home to a feverish kid. I seldom had to confront this problem. Mabel lived with us during the week, coming in early Monday morning and leaving on Friday evening to go home to her own family in Brooklyn. But every once in a while we'd have a Black Monday: one of the girls would have a temperature, and Mabel would call in sick, too. For days like that, Michael and I had an unusual pact. If he had an important meeting that morning, I would stay home until we could find a reliable babysitter. If *I* had an important meeting, *he* would stay home. It took an extraordinary man to do that in the sixties, and one very confident in his masculinity. If we both had important meetings, however, there was no question about the outcome. *I* would stay home.

Most working mothers were on the job seven days a week. We were professionals Monday through Friday from nine A.M. until whatever time we could get home; we were wives and mothers and housewives the rest of the time. And we were tired. We were almost always tired. It didn't really matter how much status you had at the office, or how much money you made. It was still the woman's job to make sure that the household ran smoothly, that the kids did their homework, that there was a good dinner on the table (even if she didn't cook it). Mary Wells Lawrence was the one who flew to Dallas every weekend to see her husband, not the other way around.

Reva Korda startled me one day by telling me she had been doing the laundry in the basement laundry room of her apartment house at eleven o'clock the night before. At that point, Reva was executive creative director of the entire agency, without question the most important woman in the place, and the highest-salaried one. "I was so tired, I started to cry," she told me. I just stared at her, incredulous. I thought I was the only one who ever felt that way.

I cried, too. I usually cried on Fridays because the weekend was coming. Mabel wouldn't be there, and many summer weekends, neither would Michael. Before we made enough money to rent a vacation home for a month, Michael played golf every Saturday. He didn't belong to a country club then, because we couldn't afford that either, so he'd leave early for some public golf course in New Jersey, and I knew he'd be gone all day. I cried because I'd be alone taking care of the kids. I cried because I was so tired. Everybody else got days off; I never did. Most of all, I cried because without the aura of my job, I felt diminished, a nonentity. I had nothing to say.

I knew a lot of full-time moms, and heard them chatting away at cocktail parties, telling funny little anecdotes about toilet training, and charming tales of domestic mishaps. They seemed at ease with the idea that life at home with kids was great stuff for conversations. I could not offer up a single charming story about child rearing or housekeeping, so I simply became a mute.

I'd square my shoulders and take Kate and Jenny to the playground in Central Park, promising myself I wouldn't look at my watch until I thought it was at least eleven, almost time for lunch and naps. We'd go on the slides and the swings and the seesaws and climb the climbing bars and play in the sandbox. Finally, when I was sure we'd been in the park for hours,

I would peek at my watch and see that it was nine forty-five. And I'd cry.

Women in the fifties were trapped in that "problem that had no name," as Betty Friedan called it in *The Feminine Mystique.* That mystique held that women were destined to get married and bear children and tend their households. They had no individual identity but existed merely as "J.R.'s wife" or "Johnny's mother." There was no "I."

Working women in the sixties, especially women with children, were racked with guilt pretty much all the time. When we were with our husbands and children, we felt guilty about not being at the office. When we were at the office—not all the time, but at into-the-night creative sessions or all-weekend crashes for a new business pitch—we felt guilty about not being at home. Most of my working friends told me they reproached themselves most about their husbands because of the three priorities, they were the lowest rung.

It was different for me. As I've said, my ranking was job first, husband second, children third. And Michael came in a very high second. I have never analyzed this very closely, but I probably reasoned that unless I gave it a lot of attention, my career might go away. And unless I gave Michael a lot of attention, *he* might go away. But the children would hang in. I always felt guilty about not giving them enough attention, though. I still feel that way.

There's one simple reason why I could give my children low priority: Mabel. She is a pivotal figure in my life, and as much mother to Kate and Jenny as I am. Maybe more. She came to us in 1963 and stayed for thirty-two years.

Mabel's name is really Carmen Dyce, but Mabel is what they call a "pet name" in Jamaica, so as Mabel she came to us, and Mabel she remains. In Jamaica they raise children with equal amounts of discipline and love, and lots of both. That's the way she raised our daughters, who called her May-May, piling one nickname on top of another. Back home in the town of Race Course, outside of Kingston, Mabel was a serious runner as a teenager, so good she almost made the Olympics. She taught school for some years, then opted to come to the United States, where she could earn more money. A single mom, Mabel made the tough decision to leave her son, Locksley, in Jamaica with her mother; she felt he would get a better education under the English system there. She came up to share an apartment with Jamaican relatives in Brooklyn, and ran a persuasive "situation wanted" ad in *The New York Times* for "housekeeper." Our former housekeeper had retired; Kate was three and I was pregnant with Jenny and needed help fast. Mabel and I met and agreed on a salary, and she started the next day.

We settled into a routine. Mabel came in on Monday morning, spent the week with us, and left on Friday evening to go home to Brooklyn. During the summer, Mabel and the girls stayed by themselves at our Westhampton Beach home, and she stayed on many of the weekends. I paid her extra for that, but not much.

Mabel read to Kate and Jenny, recited nursery rhymes, helped them with their homework, and took them to the pediatrician and the dentist. She also gave them fierce instructions in etiquette. One evening we invited a good friend, a world-famous architect, to family dinner, and Jenny, then four, asked him politely to take his elbows off the table.

As the girls became teenagers, Mabel became more strict than ever and kept an eagle eye on her charges. She wanted them under her nose when they weren't at school. As a result, she ran a kind of continuous open house for the girls' friends, with after-school snacks in the New York City apartment, and homemade ice cream at the Westhampton Beach house. (Her fresh peach is divine.) There were always gaggles of young women at our homes and, as the girls matured, scores of young men. Mabel would have been an ideal Bucknell housemother; decorum always reigned.

Many women who have had a dozen housekeepers or more ask me enviously for the secret to our long relationship. Mabel and I respected each other and each other's territory. When she gave the kids a directive, I was careful not to countermand it. In addition to raising the children, Mabel was responsible for the apartment, and I didn't interfere. She did the shopping, the cleaning, the cooking—everything.

Once a week, Mabel did her famous thorough housecleaning. She would start at the furthest reach of the apartment with a good stiff broom and sweep all debris before her until she got to the kitchen. By that point, her mound was usually larger than she was. Today, Jenny cleans her home exactly the same way.

Thursdays were official wash days. Mabel would come in and strip the beds, strip the bathrooms, strip the kitchen, strip everything in sight, all at high speed. Michael always left for the office early on Thursdays. He feared that one day she would strip him, too.

Mabel was a plain Jamaican cook when she joined us, a gourmet chef by the time she left. Her signature dish, the one our guests oohed and aahed over, was an appetizer: eggs scrambled with crème fraîche and topped with caviar, served in half an eggshell and eaten with a demitasse spoon. Cutting the shells in half without shattering them was an exercise in dexterity and patience. Mabel says those eggs alone have earned her a place in heaven.

Years went by; Mabel's son, Locksley, spent summers with us in Westhampton and became a surrogate son and brother. When he finished high school, Mabel brought him to New York for college. He went on to a long and successful career in administration at the New York University Medical Center, becoming one of the top administrators at New York University Hospital. After both our daughters finished college and had apartments of their own, Mabel volunteered that perhaps I wouldn't need her any longer. "My God, Mabel, don't leave me," I begged. "What would I do without you?" It wasn't until Michael retired in 1995 and we moved to the Westhampton house that Mabel retired, too, and moved to Florida. We invited her up several times a year, so she could visit with Locksley, see her two granddaughters, and spend some time with us.

When Michael died at New York Hospital in 2002, there were just four of us with him: Kate, Jenny, Mabel, and I. At the memorial service, Locksley was one of the three eulogists. When Jenny was married eighteen months later, Allen, the groom, raised a toast to his "two mothers-in-law." Mabel was the mother who sobbed through the entire ceremony. And, again, Locksley was one of the official participants. When I had surgery for colon cancer in 2007, Mabel was here to take me to the hospital, take me home from the hospital, and stay with me until she was satisfied I was on the mend.

She is the most devout member of our family. She has a little "prayer closet" to which she retires several times a day. If Kate or Jen or I have a really important favor we're asking of God, we get Mabel to intercede. Her prayers are powerful and very often answered.

Wasn't I jealous of her, people ask me, envious of the fact that she took over the maternal role in the family? No. Mabel was my lifeline. And in many ways, although she is only one year older than I am, she was my mother, too.

Because of Mabel, I was able to give Michael more attention than most working moms give their husbands, probably even more than a stay-at-home mom would have time for. So I always assumed Michael knew my career was essential to me and would never dream of asking me to give it up. Yet on the day he became a partner in his architectural firm, he immediately walked the fifteen blocks to Ogilvy, arrived in my office unannounced, and told me his news. "Now you can quit working," he said. Of course he knew I wouldn't do that, but he needed to tell me that, as far as he was concerned, I *could.*

As I became a well-known advertising woman, largely due to the "I Love New York" campaign I headed, invitations came in for me to speak at tourism conferences all over the country and around the world. Michael enjoyed hobnobbing with the rich and famous, the private jets, the exotic destinations, the storied villas.

I was also asked to join a number of boards, both for-profit and pro bono. A year after Michael finished his term on the board of directors of the American Institute of Architects, I was elected to that body as one of their two non-architect public directors. The other public director was Jonas Salk. I asked Michael how he felt about attending these gatherings as a spouse. "Privileged," he said, and kissed me. "And besides, I get to hang out with the thirty-eight other spouses. And they're all women."

The seventies were a wonderful time for me, but in many ways it was a difficult decade for women, because we were constantly being told that we "had it all," and could do *everything.* And of course we couldn't. At this point we not only had careers and husbands and children to juggle, we had to march for more rights for women. The Equal Rights Amendment came up again during the Jimmy Carter presidency, and prominent men and women formed the Business Council for the ERA. Mary Wells was invited to join the council but declined, and suggested that I could represent Wells Rich Greene in her stead. I didn't care much about the amendment, feeling women had to earn their equal status instead of having it legislated for them, but I was thrilled to rub shoulders with all those corporate bigwigs. The council even elevated me to the steering committee, probably because they thought advertising was the same thing as public relations, and that I might be able to get them favorable press coverage.

The Carters invited the council leadership to come to Washington for lunch and to hear President Carter speak on behalf of the amendment. I presented myself at the White House gate. The guard asked to see my invitation, and I realized I hadn't thought to bring it along. "I'll have to ask for identification," he said. I promptly whipped out my American Express card. The guard raised his eyebrows in surprise. "I'm afraid that here at the White House, we do not accept American Express. Let me see your passport." I told him rather indignantly that I didn't travel from New York to Washington with a passport. "Okay," he finally conceded, "your driver's license will have to do." I confessed that I didn't have a driver's license because I had never learned to drive. An *American citizen* who didn't know how to drive! Clearly, his expression indicated, he was dealing with a potentially dangerous anarchist. They were about to haul me away and frisk me when someone I knew on the Carter staff vouched for me. The guard let me through and muttered as I passed, "Next time, carry a passport."

The Equal Rights Amendment was defeated, chiefly by women, especially the vociferous Phyllis Schafly, who convinced women that we were all going to have to share urinals and play football. Most of us who had worked for its passage shrugged and went on about our business. We knew equality was heading our way, with or without an amendment.

As I write, *Mad Men* has yet to air season five. As of now, however, there are no working mothers at Sterling Cooper or Sterling Cooper Draper Pryce. The secretaries are all young and single; when they marry, they soon quit work and stay home. Yet there must have been mothers who had to work, and who were holding down clerical jobs to help support their families. Where are they? In a series that is praised for its historical accuracy, this seems like a significant omission.

But I have to accuse myself of the same sin. My sister, Susan, spotted it when she read an earlier version of this chapter. "Wait," she said. "There is a whole piece missing. You've been writing only about mothers who had big career goals, women who were copywriters or account executives, women like you who *wanted* to work. What about the mothers who *needed* to work, who had to take jobs as typists and secretaries and file clerks? Where were they at Ogilvy & Mather?"

"I'm sure they were there," I said. "But I don't remember any of them."

"Ah," Susan said softly. "They were invisible."

CHAPTER 5

The Three-Martini Lunch and Other Vices

Everyone I know who worked on Madison Avenue in the 1960s complains that *Mad Men* exaggerates the liquor consumption. "It's not at all realistic," one account man complained to me. "We never drank in the *morning*."

True, most people I knew didn't drink in the morning, but there were two exceptions. When my husband quit smoking in 1966, he had an ice-cold beer with his coffee every morning for a week. He said he needed it to get his heart started. And there was one client who turned into a regular morning drinker because of me. Hank worked on the "I Love New York" business for the State Tourism Department. Almost every Monday morning we'd get on the train together in New York and make the two-and-a-half-hour trip to Albany to meet with various legislators. Hank was always hungover on Monday mornings, and one day was especially painful. I took pity on him and went to the train's café car and brought him a Bloody Mary. "Hair of the dog," I told him. He had never encountered a Bloody Mary before, and thought it was heaven. He had two more before we got to Albany, and by the end of the day was well on his way back into an even worse hangover.

Hank became a Bloody Mary aficionado. He discovered that Wells Rich Greene had well-stocked liquor cabinets and a superb staff who could whip up any drink at any hour. He began calling early morning meetings at the agency, and always presided with a Bloody Mary in hand. I learned later that the staff referred to him as "Jane's Bloody client."

We didn't drink in the morning, but, for sure, the rest of the day, most people drank most of the time. Viewers of *Mad Men* ask me in some disbelief if we really drank like that at lunch. It was the custom then to drink before eating, during eating, and after eating. Then everybody came back to their offices at about two o'clock and went to work. Those lucky enough to be finished by five and able to leave went to a bar and started right in again. "How did we do it?" I ask my old buddies. They stare at me and shake their heads in wonder. "That's what I keep asking myself," they say. "How did we do it?" Jerry Della Femina says we got away with it because our coworkers and our clients had just as much to drink at lunch as we did, so it was a level playing field. I think it was also because we were so young and healthy and stupid that we didn't think booze or cigarettes—or anything—could kill us.

Looking back, it seems to me that the men I worked with went out to lunch every day, but the women didn't—probably a combination of work ethic and weight control. I remember one long morning at Ogilvy when the client turned down three television storyboards we presented. The account team and the creative director took the client out for lunch; I stayed at the office and worked with an art director. By the time they all came back, we had a new concept to show, complete with storyboard. The client approved it.

Often, it was the men in our working lives who invited women to "have another." Linda Bird Francke, when she was still doing secretarial work at Young & Rubicam, reported to creative supervisor Bob Higbee, who took her to lunch a lot. "We'd start with martinis and end with Rusty Nails—that's a combination of scotch and Drambuie—and go back to work." "How on earth did you manage to go back to work after that?" I asked. "I think what saved us," Linda said thoughtfully, "is that we didn't have wine in between."

Daisy Nieland Sinclair told me that she, too, started her career at Y&R, and, coincidentally, she worked as a secretary to Bob Higbee a year or two after Linda did. Higbee took her out for lunch a lot, too, and they always started with martinis. "And ended up with Rusty Nails?" I asked knowingly. "Oh no," she said. *Well,* I thought. *Mr. Higbee was cutting down.* "No," Daisy continued. "I didn't like scotch, so after lunch we always had stingers."

I suspect that Bob Higbee didn't drink more at lunch than many of his peers, and he must have been a pretty good copywriter: David Ogilvy later hired him away from Y&R. He was an extremely important mentor to both Linda and Daisy. He encouraged Linda to hone her creative skills and become a copywriter. "He gave me a copy of Strunk and White's *Elements of Style,*" Linda recalls, "which I still keep on my desk. The inscription reads: 'For Linda Bird Mackenzie, wife, bon vivant, Y&R copywriter, with affection and hope, Bob Higbee,

June 7, 1962.' He was one of the most supportive and influential men in my professional life and a lovely man to boot. I adored him."

When Bob went from Y&R to Ogilvy, he took Daisy with him and urged her to move up from secretarial work. "I think he knew I wasn't cut out for copywriting," Daisy said, "but when a job opened up in the casting department, he encouraged me—no, that's wrong, he *badgered* me—to apply for it." Daisy eventually headed the department.

Daisy's mention of stingers stirred memories for me. They are a pleasant-tasting but lethal concoction of white crème de menthe and brandy. I had them only once in my life, but they made a lasting impression on me. Michael and I were in our brief, four-month courting period. We met in March of 1957, on a blind date arranged by his brother, Peter.

Peter Maas had been a writer at *Look* magazine when I was working at Time Inc., and we'd met a few times. He called me one Friday to tell me his kid brother was coming to town and needed a date for the following night. I didn't want to be a last-minute, last-resort choice, so I told Peter coolly that I already had plans. "I'm really sorry," Peter said. "Mike is a lieutenant in the Marine Corps, and he's only going to be in New York for two days." "I'll break my date," I said. "It's the patriotic thing to do."

Michael arrived, resplendent in his uniform, at my bachelor-girl apartment. He was stationed in San Diego, where he was aide-de-camp to the commanding general; as an aide he seemed to warrant more gold braid than the average lieutenant. I was enthralled.

We joined Peter and his date for dinner, then went on to a club where we had more drinks and watched belly dancers.

By the time Michael escorted me home, it was two in the morning, so I invited him up for scrambled eggs and coffee. We opened the refrigerator, which was starkly empty except for one egg and a bottle of champagne. We scrambled the egg, drank the champagne, and made love. It was my first time. Just before we went to sleep, Michael made a pronouncement: "You and I are going to be married." "Thank God," I said to myself. To Michael I said simply, "Yes." I had fallen head over heels in love with him. The next day he flew back to San Diego and the Marines, and the matter seemed to slip his mind. So I flew out to San Diego in April on the pretext of interviewing some zookeeper as a possible contestant on *Name That Tune.* Michael and I had a lovely weekend, and on Sunday I was scheduled to take the late-night flight back to New York.

Michael took me to dinner at the officers' club. With coffee, he suggested I might like a stinger. I didn't know what it was. "Oh, a stinger is very mild, very soothing," Michael told me. "Let me introduce you to the stinger." I think he had other introductions in mind, but suddenly, after two stingers, it was time to leave for the airport.

This was 1957, before jets were common for commercial use. The prop plane flight from San Diego to New York took about nine hours. I waved good-bye to Michael, stashed my hat, fastened my seat belt, and slept until the moment we touched down at LaGuardia the next morning. The stewardess told me we had flown through the worst turbulence she had ever encountered. Most of the passengers were violently ill. My bleary-eyed seatmate looked at me with loathing. "Jesus, lady," he said. "You sure can sleep."

Michael never plied me with stingers again, but he did fly to New York in June to repeat his proposal, and we married in August.

One of the legendary drinkers at Ogilvy was a television producer. Vince was a good-looking, tough-talking Italian, reputed to be a street fighter. Every evening he would hold court at his favorite bar, drink four or five martinis on the rocks with a twist, and never miss a beat. "One more of the same, Sammy," he'd keep telling his pal the bartender. Even the biggest drinkers at the agency were awed. One evening I joined the crowd at Vince's bar and sat there deciding what to order. His martini looked very crisp and cold, so I picked it up without even asking permission and took a sip. Vince looked at me pleadingly and whispered, "Don't give me away." He was drinking water.

Almost all the executives on *Mad Men* keep bottles or decanters of liquor in their offices, and offer drinks at all hours of the day. Sometimes people come in and help themselves to a morning shot. Lots of the senior men at Ogilvy kept liquor in their offices, but that was for drinks at the end of a long day or when people were working late. I don't recall one single instance of anyone having a shot in the morning. All senior staffers—vice presidents and above—had easy access to liquor anytime because we were members of the executive dining room, known as Rose's Room in honor of Rose, who presided as chef at lunch every day. There was no bartender, but the place had every liquor imaginable, a selection of good wines, and fashionable waters. All this, every day if we liked, was on the house. It must have cost the agency a fortune. The first time I was there, I reached for a bottle of Perrier. The president of the agency urged me to have a scotch instead. "It's cheaper."

When I first became an officer, there were only two of us women who were vice presidents, so Rose's Room was predominantly a male bastion. However, members were allowed to invite guests, so there were occasionally other women in the room. David Ogilvy insisted that the place be run like a good men's club: nobody was allowed to bring paperwork, and talking business was discouraged. From the first, women in Rose's Room were treated with utter courtliness. I'm sure many of the men wished that like a good men's club, the agency would have a separate dining room for ladies.

Clients were also welcomed into Rose's Room, if they were clients we liked and respected. At one lunch, I was seated next to a client whose name, title, and corporate connection escaped me in the babble of conversation. He and I began chatting, and I admitted I hadn't caught his name. "Jim," he said. "Jane," I replied. Jim mentioned he happened to know that Ken Roman and I were writing a book together, and there was a chapter on how to be a better client. "I'd like to know more about that. Who is the client you most enjoy working with? And why?"

Suddenly, a hush fell on Rose's Room, and everybody was looking at me. I took a deep breath. "There are lots of clients I like, but the one who is most consistent in getting good creative work from the agency is General Foods."

My unknown companion looked thoughtful and asked why. *He's probably from Lever Brothers,* I worried, but I plunged on. "Because the people we work with at GF really trust us creative people. They never bully us, the way some clients do.

And every now and then, they'll tell us they don't agree with a creative direction we've suggested but are going to support spending the money to test it, anyway. So we'll work all night to do a good job for them."

"I'm going to remember that advice," he said, and shook my hand. Later, Bill Phillips, head of the General Foods business at Ogilvy, told me the mystery client was Jim Ferguson, then head of GF's Birds Eye division, soon to become corporate chairman and CEO. "Why don't you eat lunch in Rose's Room every day," Bill suggested.

All officers had keys to Rose's Room, so we could go there anytime and help ourselves to whatever we wanted to drink. One creative director I worked for preferred to drink in his office while having his hair cut. Some evenings, he would liberate a bottle of scotch from Rose's supply, get ice out of the little refrigerator in his office, and invite his copy group heads in for a drink. We'd sit around his office, drink, brainstorm ideas, and watch Emil trim his hair. I thought drinking while watching a haircut bordered on theater of the absurd, but I also suspected I might be a bit provincial.

Most of the time, when anybody at Ogilvy wanted a drink after work, we'd go across the street to Rattazzi's. You would find many of the different strata of Ogilvy life there, with a few exceptions. The most junior people didn't have the money to hang out at bars after work unless somebody was treating. Media people didn't come because they worked every night. Nobody was there from personnel (what came to be called human resources) because they couldn't risk being caught up in the sexual liaisons that so often resulted from after-hours at Rattazzi's. But everybody else was there. Because talking business was frowned on in Rose's Room, some of the senior executives went to Rattazzi's for a drink or two before lunch to wrap up a business discussion. Then they would adjourn to Rose's Room, where the food was better. David Ogilvy would show up at Rattazzi's on occasion, but never to drink; he would come only when he was looking for one of his copywriters.

People congregated in distinct groups: account people, creative people, research people. The head of personnel, Fran Devereux, went there only once, persuaded by friends to have a drink to celebrate her birthday. A charming if slightly tipsy Ogilvy account supervisor asked her to have another. They were married six months later.

Although there was lots of sex on film shoots, I recall very little drinking. Too much was at stake. Usually, the agency and the production house had just one day, or at the most two, to get the thirty-second commercial "in the can." Any delay could kick you into overtime; or "golden time" as the union crews called it, because it doubled or tripled their hourly wages. I am told that the model for "The Man in the Hathaway Shirt," George Wrangel (said to be a displaced White Russian baron), would take a nip every hour during print shoots for Hathaway. "By noon, we'd have to prop up the Baron's arm," a member of the production staff remembers. "By midafternoon, we'd have to prop up the Baron."

There were long stretches at Ogilvy when nobody went out to lunch, nobody raided Rose's Room for scotch, nobody drank a drop. When we were preparing for a big, important client presentation or making a new business pitch, we all worked flat out, including at night and on weekends. I know we didn't drink, and I remember vividly what we ate. Cold pizza. It was hot when delivered, but by the time we finished our creative chores, the cheese was always congealed and the pepperoni shriveled.

For many of the characters on *Mad Men,* the drinking is without question out of control. I don't remember it being out of control ever at Ogilvy, although I was certainly naïve about the symptoms. On the show, Don Draper drinks all the time, and is apparently getting worse as the series unfolds. Roger Sterling, despite two heart attacks, continues to drink and smoke heavily. Betty Draper seems to be sinking into alcoholism during the breakup with Don. The only problem drinker who seeks help is copywriter Freddy Rumsen. He is fired by the Sterling Cooper agency but reappears fifteen months later, a recovering alcoholic, and is rehired by Sterling Cooper Draper Pryce. Peggy Olson is supportive, but most of his other colleagues view his sobriety with scorn or bafflement.

In all my time in advertising, I was aware of only one person who had a severe drinking problem. He was a creative director, and a brilliant one—until noon every day. He drank so much at lunch that he spent the afternoons in a kind of stupor. Everyone who worked with him knew that you had to make appointments with him in the morning. He always returned to his office after lunch, and if somebody not in the know came to him with a creative request, he would beam benignly and say something incoherent. Word got around fast. I have lost contact with him, but if he is still alive, I hope he got help.

I was not aware of any woman with a drinking problem, although, again, that was clearly naïveté on my part. There was a definite double standard for alcohol consumption, so women had to do serious drinking in private. The liquor industry still followed an unwritten law that no women could appear in their advertisements. David Ogilvy broke this taboo with ads for Puerto Rican rum, but for years afterward women still could not be shown in an advertisement drinking, or even holding a glass. Jo Foxworth, another of the rare women in the Advertising Hall of Fame, wrote "Nine Commandments for Career Women." The Eighth Commandment was "Thou shall not match martinis with the men." Jo added, "Some women can drink some men under the table, but a man under the table can still be dangerous."

Ogilvy creative director Joel Raphaelson, looking back, believes there were probably more alcoholics than we knew. He points out that in a company the size of Ogilvy, statistics suggest there would have been some fifty alcoholics. "Alcoholism never came up as a matter that senior managers should be informed on—how to recognize it and how to treat it." One creative supervisor, an alcoholic, who had reported to Joel, ended up shooting himself. "Wc should have done something to help," Joel says ruefully, "but we didn't."

The characters in *Mad Men* smoke even more incessantly than they drink; and they smoke wherever they are. The gynecologist Peggy Olson visits to get birth control pills even smokes in the examining room. At the beginning and end of every tense scene, all the participants smoke hungrily. Anne Wallach, still a smoker herself, says it looks phony. "They stick the cigarettes right in the center of their mouths." I know actors love to have a prop to play with; it helps them convey a particular emotion. Most of the cast apparently studied at the Bette

Davis school of cigarette smoking; they flare their nostrils and take immensely long drags. There's constantly a lot of stage business about clicking lighters and hunting for matches.

Those of us who were smokers—and in the sixties that was still most of us—know that smoking is a habit the smoker usually isn't aware of. Jerry Della Femina, who smoked three packs a day, said that he would often have one cigarette in his hand, another in the ashtray. During one client presentation, he put his cigarette down for just a moment in order to draw something on a blackboard, and tried to light the piece of chalk.

I smoked two packs a day and told myself that I enjoyed every cigarette, but I really chain-smoked without noticing that I was doing it. One day, as we were leaving a long Procter & Gamble meeting in Cincinnati, I noticed that the big ashtray on the conference room table was overflowing with butts. *My goodness,* I thought, *we've been doing a lot of smoking here today.* Then I realized that I, the only woman in the room, had also been the only smoker. It was one of the revelations that finally helped me quit.

And I don't know why I think it's so terrible for the gynecologist to smoke in the examining room. Just an hour after Kate was born, a nurse brought this tiny, five-pound infant to me in my hospital bed. I cradled her in one arm and smoked a cigarette. Other horrifying or mortifying moments include me as one of a bevy of bridesmaids, cramped together in a car heading for the church. There was enough tulle and net to create a firestorm, but I had to light a cigarette. And once, at a black-tie fund-raiser for the Girl Scouts, I lit up at the jam-packed cocktail reception and burned a hole in a woman's evening gown.

To make me feel even more terrible, she was a clerical assistant at the Scouts' New York office, and I was sure that was her only fancy dress. I offered to reimburse her, but she wouldn't hear of it.

The first episodes of *Mad Men* were about the agency's all-important Lucky Strike account. This was 1960; the government was clamping down on claims like "low-tar," and *Reader's Digest* had just published an article linking smoking and lung cancer. Most people smoked on, and so did I. More and more reports were issued about the dangers of smoking, and Michael quit. Cold turkey. Except for the first week and the beers at breakfast, he had no problem. He began to tell me he had never realized how awful smokers smelled. I got the hint and decided to quit immediately. It was an agonizing eleven-year process.

I went to see a psychologist, who advertised that in just one session of hypnosis, he could get anyone to quit. Hypnosis had worked wonderfully for me before. I had chosen obstetricians who used the technique, and both Kate and Jenny were born while I, without benefit of anesthesia, was blissfully hypnotized and thought I was lying on a beach in the Bahamas. The psychologist put me under easily and gave me a little mantra to recite. Some forty-five minutes later, I left his office repeating, "I will never smoke again. I will never smoke again." As soon as I left his waiting room, I lit a cigarette.

I decided to go cold turkey. After all, that worked for Michael, and I had as much discipline as he, didn't I? I really did try. I stopped buying cigarettes, but I would accost strangers in a supermarket or on the street and ask pitifully, "Could you please sell me one cigarette for a dime?" (Cigarettes were then about sixty cents a pack.) Smokers always took pity on me and offered a cigarette without taking the money.

That winter of my attempted quitting, weekends were the worst. We now owned a tiny doll's house of a weekend home in Westhampton Beach. During the day on Saturday, I would steal drags while doing errands. After dinner, as we watched television together, one of the ever-present anti-smoking commercials always came on, and my daughters would look at me adoringly. *Our mom has quit.* When I couldn't stand it any longer, I'd excuse myself and go to the bathroom and lock the door. There was only one little dormer window, high up over the toilet. So I would stand on the toilet bowl, open the window and let in the arctic blast, light a cigarette, put my mouth as close to the window as I could, and blow smoke out. It was humiliating. I finally confessed to Michael that I hadn't yet quit. "I knew that, Mops," he said. "Listerine doesn't work for residual bathroom smoke."

I kept smoking, and so did most of the people in my creative group. We were increasingly concerned about the health statistics and increasingly guilty because most of our spouses were quitting. At one point, we pooled our money and hired someone who billed himself as a motivational behaviorist. Or maybe he was a behavioral motivationalist. At any rate, he said he would help us quit. For two weeks, every Tuesday and Thursday night, we gathered in the office to listen to him. On the second Tuesday, he instructed us to throw away our cigarettes before midnight that night. I complied. The next morning, I wanted a cigarette with my first cup of coffee, wanted one even more with my second cup, quarreled with Michael, scolded the children, found fault with Mabel, and arrived at the office in a foul mood.

I decided to make the rounds and see if everybody else was doing better with quitting. My most prolific copywriter sat in her office with her head down on her typewriter, sobbing, "I will never be able to write another word." My most inventive art director was in his office, happily, roaringly, exuberantly drunk. "I don't mish smoking," he announced to me. "I don't mish it at all."

I reached the last office on the corridor and heard the reassuring sound of a typewriter. *Praise be,* I thought, *Peter is working. At least one of us is able to quit smoking without a problem.* Peter turned to see who had entered his office. He was sucking furiously on a baby's pacifier.

It took me another ten years before I really quit, in 1977, when I went to SmokEnders and took their twelve-week course. The final impetus wasn't health concerns at all. SmokEnders asked all of its enrollees why we were quitting, and the cause was almost never fear of disease. People quit for reasons like mine. I couldn't go to the theater without yearning for the intermission, so I could go out and smoke. I was the biggest or only ashtray filler at client meetings. No, what made me quit wasn't concern for my health, it was social pressure.

SmokEnders brilliantly searched the world of addiction-stoppers, and incorporated the best. You had to wrap your cigarette pack in layers of paper and tie it up with rubber bands. Before every cigarette you smoked, you not only had to undo it all, you had to write in your journal why you needed this fix. At breakfast you had to choose between a cigarette and a cup of coffee; in the evening you were allowed a drink or a cigarette but not both. Simultaneously, as they were breaking habits, the course was making us cut down on our nicotine. By the last week, we were not only smoking fewer cigarettes, we were all smoking only the obligatory King Sanos. You had to have a pair of lungs like a bellows to get any trace of nicotine from this brand.

I quit smoking just before midnight on October 17, 1977. Following SmokEnders' advice, I flushed the last of my King Sanos down the toilet. Michael was away visiting a client; Kate, Jenny, and Mabel were all asleep. At about one o'clock, desperate for a cigarette, I ransacked every pocket and every pocketbook in the apartment. Nothing, not even loose tobacco, or I would have chewed it. Then I remembered that a late-night bar on Lexington Avenue had a cigarette machine. I ransacked the apartment again and came up with the requisite change. I got dressed, walked in pouring rain to the bar, and stood outside, holding the money ready in my fist. SmokEnders promised that if you didn't manage to quit at the end of the course, you could re-enroll free. I stood there, thinking about those endless hours of withdrawal, loathing my lack of willpower, so I threw the money into the gutter and went home. That night I promised myself that if I lived to be seventy, I would buy a whole carton of Marlboros and smoke every single one.

As a reward for quitting, Michael took me to Paris for a weekend in early December. The pungent smell of Gauloises—to me the world's most seductive cigarette—almost did me in, but I remembered my seventieth-birthday promise. As I write, I am seventy-nine. I haven't bought that carton yet.

Mad Men hasn't yet made a big deal of marijuana. But, again, as I write, the series has not yet begun season five. On television it is still 1965; Woodstock and the entry of pot smoking into our national consciousness is four years in the future. Pot is barely referred to on the show until season three, when Peggy smokes it with Kinsey and Smitty. Although she says she feels "very high," she is the only one of the three to come up with a creative idea. And she seems very lucid as she heads back into her office and tells her worried, disapproving secretary that everything is all right.

I knew pot existed because before I met Michael, during my early days on *Name That Tune,* I was dating a tenor sax player. He played with jazz bands, so we hung out with jazz musicians, and it was right out of *A Star Is Born.* After they played for the paying guests, the band played for themselves and their own pleasure, often until sunrise. I was twenty-three years old, fresh from Bucknell and Cornell, and dizzy at the idea of being with a jazz-playing, tough-talking Italian at four A.M. at some club in Greenwich Village where the air was filled with funny-smelling smoke. Johnny never offered me a drag, and I never asked him for one.

By the 1970s, the cooler, younger creative types on Madison Avenue were all smoking joints. Jerry Della Femina says that, in fact, the young folks at the agencies were smoking but not drinking, and sort of smirked at the older folks still getting high on alcohol. Marijuana was illegal, of course, but most agencies looked the other way. And clients thought pot was a barometer of creativity. The more grass their copywriters and art directors smoked, the wilder the commercials they might dream up. Mary Wells writes in her autobiography that she often referred vaguely to problems with substance abuse to reassure her clients that their creative people were among the desirable crazies.

With all this going on quite overtly, it's odd that not one person among the dozens and dozens I interviewed admitted to smoking pot. And only one person offered a specific recollection. That woman, a senior copywriter, became annoyed at the gaggle of men who were always hanging around her assistant's desk. One evening she came out of her office, shooed them all away, and asked the secretary, "Are you in heat?" Then she realized what was happening: the young woman was dealing.

At Ogilvy the pot smoking was fairly public. There was one creative group that smoked a lot of hash, all day, every day. You caught that unmistakable pungent smell as soon as you stepped off the elevator on their floor. And it was a subject for open discussion. Ron Hoff, one of the three executive creative directors at the agency, threw a Christmas party at his bachelor apartment for all the people who worked for him—there must have been forty or fifty of us. He called us all to a meeting in a big office conference room the day before the party and implored us to drink as much as we wanted. "But for God's sake, please don't smoke grass in my apartment. I have no moral compunctions, but I'm worried about a raid." Yet today all my old Ogilvy buddies look me straight in the eye and say no, there was no pot smoking that they were aware of. Adultery and alcohol, yes. Marijuana, no.

This all stood me in good stead during our daughters'

teenage years when, like everyone else in their seventies cohort, they began experimenting with marijuana. As soon as I entered the door of our apartment, if there was pot smoking going on, I'd smell it immediately. "Who do you think I am?" I would ask my kids. "I work at an *advertising agency.* I know what you're doing."

Jenny says she and her friends even moved the smoking out to the fire escape so I wouldn't know, but I still nosed it out. She told me recently that her friends thought I was really cool, really in the know. One suggested to Jen that I must be a pot smoker myself. Jen immediately denied it, but she wanted to retain my hip image. "My mom doesn't smoke grass," she said sturdily. "I think she drops acid."

CHAPTER 6

A Different Century, a Different World

Everything in the sixties seemed to conspire to make women's lives more difficult or more uncomfortable. We wore clothing that was supposed to help us look feminine and sexually attractive but that created torture underneath. In the office, we copywriters had manual typewriters; if you needed to revise a script, you had to retype it. There were no cell phones, which made communication with children at school difficult and often impossible.

Women were expected to put a nourishing dinner on the table every night, cooked from scratch. After dinner, a working mom cleaned up, supervised the children's homework, tucked them into bed, read to them, prepared the lunches they would take to school the next day, and did the laundry. Only then might she have time to write a new headline for the print ad that was due, or watch a few minutes of *The Tonight Show* with new young host Johnny Carson.

It was more than just a different century. It was a different world.

Mad Men has caused a wave of fashion nostalgia for those nipped-in waists, pouffy skirts, and tight sheaths. Lots of women are wearing them again now, but I doubt that anybody is putting up with the kind of discomfort we endured beneath the surface. The cruelest instrument was the pointed bra, which turned your breasts into javelins. Joan Holloway is the prime example of pointed bradom. In one episode, she is seen rubbing her sore shoulder. Some viewers thought her doctor boyfriend was roughing her up, but women who lived through the sixties knew exactly what caused the pain: a tight bra strap cutting into her skin.

Panty hose hadn't been invented yet, so we wore panty girdles with suspended garters to hold up our nylon stockings. The stockings still had *seams,* which needed to be straightened a thousand times a day. The slip was yet one more layer. We carried a lot of equipment. High heels were obligatory—at work, going to and from work, even at home to do housework. Sneakers were for the tennis court. We didn't have Nike jogging shoes, because jogging hadn't been invented yet. Neither had Nike.

The appropriate outfit to wear to the office was either a sheath dress or a skirt, a tailored blouse, and a jacket, with matching shoes and white gloves. No matter what the time of year, white gloves were considered the ladylike choice. A virginal friend of mine originally from Tupelo, Mississippi, explained why she was wearing white cotton gloves in New York in January. "No man would ever rape a woman who was wearing *white gloves*!"

Of course, we all wore hats. Daisy Sinclair described dressing for a job interview in the casting department of Ogilvy &

Mather in 1964. "Never mind that it was a hot July day. I borrowed a beige shantung sheath from my mother's closet, a pair of her matching shoes with very high heels, and lots of jewelry. Long white gloves. And a hat with green velvet piping and red berries that hung from it."

Hats were not only a fashion statement, they were a status symbol. "At J. Walter Thompson, as soon as you were promoted from secretary to junior copywriter, you wore a hat in the office," says Anne Wallach. "I never took my hat off, not even in the bathroom." At JWT, men and women copywriters were divided into separate groups. The men had their own dining room, but women weren't allowed to eat there. Wallach recalls, "We were served lunch at our desks every day by waitresses who brought us dainty trays. We always ate with our hats on." Marikay Raphaelson says the same hat etiquette prevailed at Ogilvy. "Wearing a hat in the office was a badge. It proclaimed you were no longer a secretary." Secretaries never wore hats in the office; it was an unspoken taboo. Once she becomes a copywriter, Peggy Olson usually wears a hat going to and from the office, but I haven't noticed that she keeps it on at her desk. It's one of the rare bits of costuming that *Mad Men* gets wrong.

We dressed to the nines when we traveled, and travel was arduous. It took nine hours on a prop plane to get from New York to the West Coast. It took forever to fly from New York to London, and the plane stopped to refuel in someplace like Iceland. Michael took me for a belated honeymoon to England in 1959, and I remember boarding the plane for this marathon in a suit, high heels, white gloves, and a hat.

Curiously, the two most important trends of the late sixties were polar opposites: the covered-up, masculine pantsuit and the revealing, feminine miniskirt. I wore both. Michael bought them for me.

For the forty-five years of our marriage, he personally shopped for every article of clothing I wore except for underwear. His architectural eye was unerring: I tended to beiges and grays; he decked me out in vivid primary colors. And he was right. I tended to conservative styles; Michael put me in costumes that made a statement. It surprised me that I could carry them, but he was right again. After his death, I was shocked to realize how difficult it was to buy a new dress.

"She wears the pants in the family" was still a damning thing to say about a woman. We never wore pants to the office. If there was a snowstorm, you might wear slacks en route to work, but you immediately changed into a dress or a skirt. Slacks were beginning to be accepted at television shoots, though. This relaxed dress code had nothing to do with comfort; on many soundstages, the agency people needed to go up onto catwalks or ladders to view the scene from the director's point of view. Slacks merely protected our maidenly modesty.

I was the first woman at Ogilvy to wear a pantsuit to the office. It was 1965, and I caused quite a stir. Reva Korda looked at me with astonishment. "Are you on a shoot?" I tried wearing it to meet Michael for dinner at '21' one night. They were very strict about dress: men had to wear coats and ties, and the management supplied a tie and even a jacket for any man who arrived without one. But they didn't keep skirts on hand for women in pants. I was politely but firmly refused admittance. I wasn't alone. A famous actress (it may have been Marlene Dietrich) arrived at '21' in a pantsuit and was told she could not come in. She went into the ladies' room, took off the pants, and returned to the gatekeeper in just her suit jacket. '21' didn't have any rules about that; they seated her. As more and more women began wearing pantsuits at the office, David Ogilvy wrote a stern memo ordering us not to. Reva, who was wearing pantsuits herself by then, persuaded him to rescind it.

Even culottes were banned. (These were pants with legs so wide, they looked like a skirt.) One day Ellen Roman, who was the first woman to become a product manager at Clairol, wore what she considered to be a conservative culottes outfit to the office. "It was gray flannel, knee-length, with long sleeves and a high neck. They told me it was 'inappropriate.'"

The miniskirt came into style at about the same time, popularized by models like Jean Shrimpton and designers like Mary Quant, André Courrèges, and Rudi Gernreich (who also gave us the topless bathing suit). The favorite accessories with the mini were fishnet stockings and white Courrèges boots. These boots became a fashion craze in themselves. Every little girl in my daughter Jennifer's nursery school class wore them. Miniskirts also signaled that the wearer was "liberated," a radical, a hippie. My sister, Susan, who is twelve years younger than I, was attending Columbia University in 1968, the year of the nationwide student sit-ins. At Columbia, the students took over the office of the president and held the dean hostage for twenty-four hours. At the height of these protests, my studious, Phi Beta Kappa sister was peacefully walking down a street near the college when a tourist bus drove by. The guide, pointing at Susan, announced over the loudspeaker, "There goes one of them now. A genuine New York hippie, ladies and gentlemen. You can tell by the miniskirt."

As the decade wore on, the skirts got shorter and shorter. Bill Bernbach finally sent out a memo to the women at Doyle Dane Bernbach asking them to show some restraint. "I don't mind skirts getting shorter," he wrote, "but I draw the line when they are merely long *belts*."

The men of *Mad Men* dress conservatively; they wear suits to the office every day, with white shirts, narrow ties, and highly polished, lace-up shoes. Most of them wear hats. It is legend that John F. Kennedy killed the hat industry when he appeared bareheaded at his inauguration. In fact, JFK wore the traditional top hat to the ceremony, and doffed it to deliver his inaugural address. Don Draper continues to wear a hat in the mid-sixties. When he takes Betty home from the hospital with baby Gene, he gets out of the car and puts his hat on for the sixty-second walk to the house.

Jack Kennedy may have been a model for some men, but every woman in the world wanted to look like Jackie. Even Barbie wanted to look like Jackie. The doll made her first appearance in 1959 sporting a ponytail, but in 1961 Bubble Cut Barbie appeared, with a hairdo supposedly inspired by Jackie's bouffant style. Red Flare Barbie (1962) wears an outfit that might be worn by Jackie or Betty Draper. It's a red velvet "swing coat" with a white satin lining, long white gloves, a red pillbox hat, and a clutch purse. Barbie's outfits also mirrored the emerging dreams of their young owners. We started with Stewardess Barbie and Ballerina Barbie and moved on to Career Girl Barbie, in a checked tweed suit and matching hat Peggy might well wear.

Barbie and her boyfriend, Ken, are a paradigm of the social codes that governed sex in the sixties. It was good to be sexy, but bad to be overt about it. Traditionally, dolls were shaped like babies or little girls, but Barbie had *breasts.* When Kate undressed her first Barbie at the age of eight or nine, Michael was shocked. A year later, someone gave her a Ken doll, and she was about to strip him down for a change of costume. "No, no, don't undress him," Michael cried, and fled from the room. He needn't have worried. Ken is sexless. He and Barbie are perhaps the ideal sixties couple; they can pet, but not consummate.

The office technology seemed cutting-edge to us, but it was amazingly primitive. Think about what we *didn't* have. Computers, for openers. The Internet. Cell phones. Faxes, almost obsolete today, hadn't yet arrived. Neither had Federal Express. So if you absolutely, positively had to get a television storyboard from the New York office to a client in Los Angeles by the next morning, you put somebody from the mailroom on a red-eye flight.

The IBM Selectric typewriter was new, but only secretaries had them. You can see the secretaries on *Mad Men* carefully putting the covers on these awesome machines every night. They could correct typos, a huge boon to clerical staff. You backspaced carefully, a letter at a time, to erase errors, then retyped. Secretaries still needed carbon paper to make copies, and even the Selectric didn't ease this process. We copywriters still had manual typewriters, huge machines that clacked fiercely. I loved mine so much that I got permission to take it from Ogilvy to Wells Rich Greene. When I left WRG I asked about the typewriter. "We'll pay you to cart it away," the office manager told me. I took it.

Television was still such a strange young medium that some

creative people didn't bother to master it. Many agencies, including Ogilvy & Mather, had entire creative groups that concentrated on print, radio, and outdoor posters. David Ogilvy encouraged us all to watch more television, and feared that perhaps the ugliness of the television sets was keeping us away. Ogilvy copywriter Peter Hochstein recalls that "the average set had a ten-inch screen encased in about a cubic mile of mahogany cabinetwork." D.O. sent a memo to his fifty-dollar-a-week copy cubs and two-hundred-dollar-a-week senior writers about where they might hide their television sets to avoid social embarrassment.

"I keep my TV in the wine cellar," David advised.

Xerox machines were just coming in, and Sterling Cooper, like many offices, had one rudimentary model. It's so big that Joan fusses about where to put it, and ends up installing it in Peggy's little office. When Peggy volunteers to make copies of fliers for the Catholic Youth Organization dance, Father Gill is duly impressed by the machine. George Lois, a founder of the Papert Koenig Lois agency, created the commercial that introduced the new technology and demonstrated how easy it was to run. His spot showed a little girl visiting her father's office and running off a copy of a document. She brings it to her dad, who asks, "Which one is the original?" The networks turned the commercial down because they didn't believe the demonstration: a child couldn't possibly master that sophisticated machinery. Lois shot a second commercial and invited the network censors to watch; this time he had a chimpanzee run the machine. The networks allowed both spots to air.

Another of the rare false notes that *Mad Men* hits is the

conventional décor of the copywriters' and art directors' offices. Creative offices at most agencies were expected to look "different." When I had been at Ogilvy for about a year, I decorated my office doorway with a curtain of bamboo strips, like the beaded curtains so popular then. An account executive who came to have a meeting with me looked at my curtain and said, "I'll come in, but I won't go upstairs." I took the bamboo down. A year later, wanting to flaunt my creativity, I installed a hammock in my tiny office. The hammock, together with the big metal stanchions that supported it, took up the entire space. There wasn't even room for a desk. After a few swinging weeks, I gave it to someone who had a house in the country.

As I moved up the ranks from copywriter to copy group head and then creative director, my offices became progressively more conservative. Art directors were the ones who could go a little crazy. One man I worked with had a barber's chair in his office. As we brainstormed ideas, he would raise and lower himself; he said it helped him think. Another art director had Judy Garland's red feather fan on his drawing board; yet another plastered his walls with Abbie Hoffman handbills. In general, men were expected to be more flamboyant than women. If we invited attention, we might also seem to be inviting sex.

The business world of the sixties was ambivalent in its treatment of women. In many ways, men regarded us as tender little flowers, so it was even more shocking when they bullied us or treated us as sex objects. A man never allowed a woman to buy him a business lunch or a drink; he would have been hideously embarrassed. I didn't pick up the check to take a client out to lunch until the 1970s. How could I? I didn't have a credit card until 1972. After I left Ogilvy for Wells Rich Greene, the president of Ogilvy and I had lunch regularly. One time he would pay, next time I would. This worked very well until the day when Andrew spotted Michael Maas at a nearby table. "My God, put away your American Express card," he hissed. "I can't let your husband see you paying for me."

All women's restrooms in those halcyon days had couches, so a woman could lie down if she was having her period. Or simply having the vapors. At J. Walter Thompson, the main restroom was complete with cots, and a nurse in attendance. Menstruation was a mystery to most men; they never knew when a woman might not be able to function. During my first year in New York, I was summoned to jury duty, but I didn't serve. I didn't even have to appear to ask to be excused. Right on the form was a box you could check, explaining why you were unable to be a juror. It stated simply: "Because I am a woman."

At this point, approximately 80 percent of married women with young children stayed at home and tended to their household chores. "Housewife" was not yet the dirty word it is today. Most American women wrote it proudly as "occupation" on the 1960 census form. It was such a positive word, in fact, that Maxwell House coffee borrowed it for a television campaign. Doting husbands made coffee for their wives and told them affectionately to "be a good little Maxwell housewife." America loved it.

Household chores could be a full-time job. There was no "permanent press." Every article of clothing worn by every member of the family needed not only to be washed, it needed to be *ironed.* You washed and starched and ironed your husband's shirts. You washed and ironed the clothes your kids wore to school. You washed and *ironed* the clothes your kids wore to play in the sandbox. Of course, I had Mabel.

For most women, preparing meals was a chore unto itself, but I had Mabel. There were no microwaves and precious few dishwashers. Frozen foods had begun to appear, as had a few "instant" versions of traditional dishes (instant rice was one of the first) but they were suspect, and a housewife who prided herself on "setting a good table" would never stoop to them.

Americans traditionally had "family dinner," and talked about the events of the day: what Dad did at the office and what the kids did at school. (Mom didn't usually have much exciting news about her day.) Psychologists and sociologists proclaimed the end of family values when we all began eating dinner in front of the television set in the living room. We ate Swanson TV dinners from compartmented metal trays. To further underscore the family division, each person had his own darling little tray stand, just big enough to hold one TV dinner. The Maas family favorite was the turkey dinner: turkey, gravy and stuffing, mashed potatoes with a tiny butter lake, peas that were sharply, astonishingly green, and cranberry sauce. I thought this was so delicious, so easy, and so nutritionally balanced that on weekends, when Mabel wasn't there, I served it to my family almost every night. We didn't eat in front of the television set, though; we sat together at the dining room table. After dinner, the girls went to their rooms to do their homework (Nightingale-Bamford was a demanding school) while Michael and I went to our bedroom to watch television.

Housewives were convinced that a can of cream of mushroom soup could transform anything into a gourmet dish. We were all busily adding calories to our proteins with Shake 'n Bake (cracker crumbs) and Hamburger Helper (more cracker crumbs). Chicken Kiev was one of the most requested *New York Times* recipes of the sixties. It was chicken breast stuffed with butter, rolled in bread crumbs, and deep-fried. Imagine.

When the Drapers give a dinner party in one early episode, Betty prepares a "round-the-world menu," and announces it proudly to the guests. She tells them the rumaki is Japanese (although it's an American creation), the gazpacho Spanish, the noodles she serves with the leg of lamb German, the wine French, and the Heineken beer (an agency client) Dutch. A number of articles have pointed out that this kind of international theme was popular in the sixties, but I don't remember that. My dinner party menus were resolutely French—and this was before Julia Child.

For my birthday in 1960, Michael's parents gave me a wonderful cookbook: *Bouquet de France,* written by gourmet architect Samuel Chamberlain, who ate his way across France every year and persuaded chefs to share their most treasured recipes. So I would cook—or, more correctly, Mabel would cook—French dishes like *coq au vin* and *bœuf bourguignon,* and when guests praised them, I would airily mention that I'd learned to make them during my year living with a French family in Dijon. I even tried serving up gefilte fish from a jar as my own made-from-scratch *quenelles de brochet.* Most guests were taken in, but I noticed a few Jewish friends raised their eyebrows, so I stopped risking discovery.

We entertained guests for dinner—usually two other

couples—at least once every two weeks. I prided myself on serving a rather worldly cuisine. As I look back, I am appalled by what the calorie count must have been. The hors d'oeuvres, served in the living room with cocktails, were usually pâté with French bread or cheese balls from a fancy French bakery. The main course never included potatoes, but there was always a baguette, and always a salad course with a selection of cheeses—cow, sheep, or goat—and more French bread. Then we would move back to the living room for dessert, often an apple tart from the same bakery, and espresso. Michael would pour liqueurs, cognac, or Drambuie, or just a scotch. And we would sit and drink. And smoke. And smoke. And smoke.

There was only one telephone in our big Park Avenue apartment, on the bedside table, with an extension in the kitchen. If our dinner guests needed to call their babysitter, they had to stand in our kitchen or sit on our bed. Next to questions about sex in the sixties, the greatest current curiosity is how we ever managed to communicate without cell phones, e-mail, or texting. For one thing, there were pay phones everywhere—not just on street corners, but in bars, delis, grocery stores, and dry cleaners. You simply deposited your ten cents. Strange as it seems, I don't remember being involved in a single mishap caused by the lack of a telephone. Staying in touch with far-flung friends was more difficult; long-distance was expensive and international calls prohibitively so. We wrote letters.

There were only three television networks, mostly showing black and white, and no cable channels. Between midnight and six A.M. there wasn't anything on television except a test pattern. For news, music, or entertainment during those hours, you turned on the radio. NBC was the leader in offering color because its parent company, RCA, was making color sets; the more color programming they provided, the more sets they would sell. ABC and CBS lagged in the color competition.

If you wanted to see a movie, you went out to a movie theater. Only toward the end of the sixties did all the networks realize that Americans had an appetite for old movies. CBS launched *Saturday Night at the Movies*, and NBC and ABC followed with "nights" of their own. There was no way to watch a movie of your choice at home unless you were like Norma Desmond of *Sunset Boulevard* and had your own screening room.

And what were we watching on those ugly sets? *Bonanza* ruled the decade, together with *Gunsmoke, Wagon Train,* and *Have Gun—Will Travel.* Early sixties television was studded with male celebrities hosting their own comedy shows—Jack Benny, Red Skelton, Dick Van Dyke, Danny Thomas. The late sixties tilted more toward women, perhaps a sign of the times. Lucille Ball was back, without Desi, in *The Lucy Show,* and Carol Burnett arrived. Patty Duke, Donna Reed, and Doris Day had their own shows, and Elizabeth Montgomery starred in *Bewitched.* The popular quiz show *What's My Line?* had never gone off the air during the scandal. The focus was on the witty panelists in their evening attire, and the most a contestant could win was fifty dollars. The network obviously felt that less prize money helped everyone avoid temptation. Gradually, though, game shows with big-money prizes began to creep back on air. Contestants today can make a million dollars on any number of shows.

The folks at Sterling Cooper eat at some of New York's finest restaurants. Don takes Rachel Menken for drinks to try to win her department store account; the zebra-striped wall treatment gives us a clue that it's El Morocco. When the senior officers entertain clients or each other, they generally choose a restaurant like La Grenouille or the Four Seasons, both still very much with us today, or Lutèce, long gone. The troops congregate at less expensive hangouts such as P.J. Clarke's. I am surprised that the series still hasn't recognized '21.' Certainly Roger and Don would eat lunch there regularly. The two restaurants Michael and I loved best were '21' and the Four Seasons.

When the Four Seasons opened in 1959, author and critic Craig Claiborne gave it a rave review in *The New York Times.* He admitted it was expensive, with lunch for two about twenty-five dollars with wine, adding that you could get a good bottle of Burgundy or Bordeaux of recent vintage for seven dollars. Those were steep prices for us in those days, so we couldn't eat there very often, but Michael entertained enough clients for his architectural firm that we were considered regulars and were given one of the coveted tables beside the pool in the main dining room.

I liked most of Michael's clients and enjoyed helping him entertain them. But we both worked hard all week and spent most of our evening and weekend time with Kate and Jenny, so it was a special treat for just the two of us to have dinner alone. One of Michael's clients had a wife who sometimes drank a bit too much during the day. Sometimes, when we had dinner plans with this couple, we would already be ensconced at our poolside table when a waiter would bring a telephone and we would learn from her husband that the lady was "indisposed." We had already ordered drinks, so it was too late to leave, and we would then enjoy a fabulous Four Seasons dinner courtesy of Haines Lundberg & Waehler, Architects.

Our other favorite restaurant was '21,' officially known as the '21' Club. The most visible of the owners, "Colonel Bob" Kriendler, had served in the Pacific in World War II and was a gung-ho Marine. Michael, who retired from the Corps with the rank of captain, was active in the reserve for several years. His older brother, Peter, used to tease him. "If the Russians attack, you'll have to go defend the '21' wine cellar."

Florence and Bob Kriendler became good friends of ours. About three months after our marriage, Michael told me he had invited a few friends for dinner. I asked how many we would be. We were living in a one-bedroom walk-up with no dining room. The "dining area" was our tiny hallway. Our seating capacity was four; six would kick us into buffet mode. It turned out that in his exuberance, proud of his new wife and his new apartment, Michael had invited twenty-five people!

I called Florence Kriendler and begged for a simple recipe. She obviously sensed my panic, and told me to have Michael take care of the drinks while I tossed a big salad and she would handle the rest. The evening of the party, a '21' van drew up outside our building. Florence Kriendler had sent me the world's largest partridge pie!

By the time Michael became a partner of his firm and I a vice president of Ogilvy & Mather, we were at '21' a lot. Actress Patricia Neal, then appearing in our Maxim coffee commercials, loved this restaurant. They always kept a jar of Maxim handy in deference to her. One night Patricia was seated at one banquette and recognized a famous man seated at the banquette next to her. She leaned over to him and asked, in that inimitable husky voice, "Have you been around the moon?" Astronaut Michael Collins, who circled the moon while Armstrong and Aldrin landed, replied charmingly, "Yes, I have, Miss Neal, but I've never been more starstruck than I am at this moment."

Yes, all of society catered to men, and restaurants did, too. There were dozens of steak houses, where the portions were gargantuan. At the Palm, two of the favorite entrees were the twenty-four-ounce rib-eye steak and the six-pound lobster. Daunted by the size of these portions, women often preferred to settle for an appetizer and a salad.

There were only two Japanese restaurants in all of Midtown, and neither of these had a sushi chef. Then Nippon opened, and my father-in-law, Carl Maas, took me there for lunch and introduced me to sashimi. I was a little afraid of my formidable mother-in-law, but Carl and I—two Pisces who shared the same birthday—were soul mates from the first. He told me I would love sashimi. As I had my first encounter with a still-quivering scallop, I hoped he was right. He was.

Nippon not only served sushi and sashimi, it had tatami rooms and a lovely little stream that wound its way around the entrance and burbled over Zen-like stones. I lost a client to that stream one day. After his usual three martinis, he discovered sake, and a little later, plum liqueur. As we were leaving, he also discovered the stream, and lay in it blissfully for several minutes while two kimonoed waitresses and I tried to haul him out. I put him in a taxi bound for Grand Central Station and a train home; he was dripping water all the way. God knows what his wife thought.

French restaurants were the only ones in New York that didn't cater to men; with their elegantly small portions, they catered to women, but only women who were slim, well-dressed, and, preferably, French. Gene Grayson took me to one of these snooty establishments for lunch as a reward for working on a successful new business pitch. Gene didn't like wine, so he ordered scotch on the rocks to drink with his main course. The restaurant refused to serve it to him. Gene demanded the check and we left before I even had a bite of their famed sole Marguery.

David Ogilvy once wanted to get female opinions on a new product and invited three of us women copywriters to dinner at a much-lauded French restaurant. The maître d' recognized David, who had recently published his bestselling *Confessions of an Advertising Man* and was something of a celebrity. He seated us at one of the best tables, produced menus with a flourish, and returned in person to take our order. "And what would Monsieur Ogilvy desire this evening?" Although David as a young man had worked as a sous-chef at the Hotel Majestic in Paris, he often paid little attention to what he ate himself. On this occasion, he wanted to dispense with the trivia of discussing food and get on to discussing advertising. He knew exactly what he wanted. "Grape-Nuts Flakes." The maître d' was not even flustered; David was also cultivating a reputation for eccentric behavior. "Alas, Monsieur Ogilvy, we have no Grape-Nuts Flakes." Well, David conceded, then he would settle for cornflakes. All of us agreed enthusiastically that cornflakes were the very thing we had been hoping for. So we sat in this hushed three-star elegance, eating cornflakes with gold spoons, trying not to crunch too loudly.

Despite all the conformity of the sixties, it was also such a time of rebellion, of emerging diversity, of fighting for rights, that I wonder why it took women so long to stand up for ourselves. The first Freedom Riders set forth in 1961, and the Stonewall riots erupted in Greenwich Village in 1969, but it wasn't until late 1970 that women took a stand. On a hot August day, ten thousand people, mostly women, marched down Fifth Avenue to celebrate the fiftieth anniversary of women's right to vote. Another Ogilvy copywriter, Gloria Guarnotta, and I were watching from the agency's windows overlooking the avenue. We didn't say a word, just ran to the elevator and out into the street, linked arms, and marched the eight blocks to Bryant Park, behind the Forty-second Street library. I had never considered myself a feminist and was secretly scornful of the bra burners with long hair under their arms, but this one time, marching with all those women, I felt exuberant. When we got to Bryant Park, Gloria and I turned around and went quietly back to work. I never marched for anything again.

Mad Men has it right about the lack of diversity at agencies in the 1960s. The only black faces you see on the show are Hollis, the elevator operator, and Carla, the Drapers' maid. Ogilvy & Mather hired its first African-American copywriter in 1968, and assigned her to my group. The day before Betty arrived, the copy chief of the agency took me aside and told me quite seriously that if I became aware of any "anti-Negro comments or gestures," I had full power to fire the perpetrator on the spot. Nobody said a word. Betty came quietly, stayed with us for about a year, wrote some effective ads, and moved on to a better job at another agency. She helped us take a big step forward.

Ogilvy had a lot of WASPs with first names like Abbott, Billings, and Whitfield, but we weren't nearly as WASPy as agencies like J. Walter Thompson and Young & Rubicam. There were a lot of Roman Catholics, too, with names like Francis Xavier. And a lot of Jews. Some of our most senior officers were Jewish, like Joel Raphaelson and Reva Korda, two of our creative leaders. Some Jews had changed their names. Andrew Kershaw, the CEO, had his name changed for him by British Intelligence, and I never knew in those days that he was Jewish. I didn't know Gene Grayson was Jewish until the day his mother died and he told me that any flowers sent to the funeral home should be for the Goldberg family.

David Ogilvy was surprised at the anti-Semitic attitude at some agencies and he "wouldn't play that game." At Ogilvy, we never discussed religion or ethnic background because you might turn up something that made everyone uncomfortable. We didn't talk about such things at Wells Rich Greene, either. By then, though, it was because such things didn't matter.

The only major gay character in the early seasons of *Mad Men* is sad, closeted Sal Romano, who is fired from Sterling Cooper not for his sexual preference but because he refuses the advances of a male client. I was dimly aware of homosexuals at Ogilvy & Mather, but I knew of only two or three people involved in television production who fit the bill. Shortly after Jim Heekin became president of the agency, he asked me into his office for a confidential chat. "Do we have too many homosexuals at this agency?" I was dumbfounded at the question, and had no answer.

As an undergraduate at Bucknell, I was virtually unaware of homosexuality. Someone asked me recently if I knew any lesbians during my four years there, and I had to answer truthfully that I did not. Not one? Not one. I became conscious of gay men (although we didn't yet use the term "gay") at the end of my senior year, when we mounted a production of Richard Brinsley Sheridan's comedy *The School for Scandal.* The period costumes for men called for lots of lace cuffs and flaunting of handkerchiefs; the mannered acting style featured lots of mincing about. One of my best friends, an actor appearing in this production, complained bitterly to me about the rampant homosexuality. Some thirty years later he told me, with some pride, that he was gay.

When I was a Fulbright scholar in France, during our orientation month in Paris I shared a tiny Left Bank hotel room and a smallish bed for two (the French call it a *lit matrimoniale*) with a charming young woman, another Fulbright, whom I met on the ship going over. Months later, she came to visit me in Dijon, where I was spending the year at the university, to tell me she was a lesbian. I shrank to the edge of the even smaller bed we shared that night, in the room I rented from the DuPont family, and assured her that this news didn't change a thing about our relationship.

In 1957, as newlyweds, Michael and I threw our first cocktail party, one that attempted to bring together our two quite different social circles. Michael was reluctant, but I was insistent. His buddies at that point were generally current or former Marine Corps officers, all spit and polish. My friends were mostly actors, and mostly the out-of-work variety. During the party, the Marines stood at one end of the living room, and the actors stood at the other. The atmosphere was funereal, the party ended early, and I cried.

"Don't cry, we'll never do this again," Michael consoled me. "No," I agreed, snuffling. "No more actors," Michael said. I agreed, and closed a whole chapter of my life. What was I thinking?

But that was the way women did things in the last century.

CHAPTER 7

Bang Bang, You're Dead (the Creative Revolution Kills)

"Who Killed Speedy Alka-Seltzer?" That's the title of a chapter in Jerry Della Femina's bestseller *From Those Wonderful Folks Who Gave You Pearl Harbor,* published in 1970 and issued again in 2010. Jerry reminds us that the creative revolution of the 1960s killed off a lot of bad advertising, including the animated character of Speedy. Mary Wells got rid of him when her new agency, Wells Rich Greene, acquired the account and she changed the campaign. Curiously enough, he has been resuscitated and stars in commercials today. The creative revolution also mercifully saw the demise of a lot of sleepy old agencies—the kind that believed the consumer was a moron—although some of them were a long time dying.

The Ted Bates Agency and its commercials for Alka-Seltzer epitomized the kind of advertising the revolutionaries despised. Hammers pounded away at the inside of an animated head while a voice-of-God announcer reported that Anacin cured headaches three ways. This old style of advertising often depended on repetition; the commercials, like the one for Anacin, banged home one fact, over and over again. Consumers complained that these spots were intrusive and noisy. Advertisers kept running them because they worked.

The kind of advertising they create at Sterling Cooper, or even Sterling Cooper Draper Pryce, is more hard-sell precreative revolution style. Don Draper's slogan for Lucky Strike—"It's Toasted"—is an example of what we call a "preemptive claim." You say something your competition could just as easily claim, only you say it first, you keep on saying it, and you end up owning it. Most cigarette companies "toasted" their tobaccos; Lucky Strike was simply the first to advertise it. The slogan has a lot of taste appeal, but the process doesn't really affect the taste, and certainly doesn't make the cigarettes less life-threatening.

The advertising of the creative revolution was characterized by *irreverence;* the product was no longer the holy grail. Historians agree that it started with Doyle Dane Bernbach and Volkswagen. DDB, the so-called "Jewish agency" located in the unfashionable West Forties, fired the opening salvo of the revolution with "Lemon." This print ad was the first time in history a car maker admitted that once in a while it turned out a substandard car that would have to be discarded. DDB next ran a full-page ad in *The New York Times* showing just a little photo of the VW at the bottom. The headline challenged every American belief about car size. It was: "Think small."

David Ogilvy and his agency were somewhere in between the old school and the new school. David believed in giving consumers *intelligent* advertising, full of important facts. But David never joined the revolution, which focused more and more on television. He was a master of *print* advertising, but admitted freely he knew little and cared little about TV. So the agency's commercials were sometimes "old" and sometimes "new," depending on the age of the people who created them.

Bill Bernbach, as I've said, is widely acknowledged as the one who started the tradition of a copywriter and an art director working together on every ad. I believe this practice had a more profound impact than most advertising historians acknowledge. Almost overnight, advertising improved. It wasn't so much the fact that a *writer* was working with an *art director.* It was the *twoness* that made the difference, two heads focusing on the problem instead of just one. They could have been two account executives, or two research directors, or two clients for that matter, as long as they understood the assignment.

Two people meant that you couldn't settle on a solution so easily; it was harder to say good enough was good enough. One member of the team might come up with an idea. His teammate could turn it down, or build on it to make it better. The first person might add an additional fillip. And so on.

Having a partner introduced healthy creative competition. It made you ashamed to offer up a tired old cliché or a retread of somebody else's advertising. Having a cool young partner also made you wary about treating the product as though it were the second coming, because the times demanded impertinence.

Flippancy was one cornerstone of the creative revolution; honesty was another. It was *honest*—although unheard of—to admit your car rental company was not number one. DDB did that for Avis with the campaign: "Avis is only #2. We try harder." That slogan not only galvanized the Avis employees to live up to it, it made the people at Hertz feel kind of sheepish. Consumers began paying attention to the new advertising. So did advertisers. So did the advertising industry.

Many of the more traditional agencies thought the new wave of ads was a disgrace. Over at Sterling Cooper, a group looks at the "Lemon" ad. Don Draper sums up the reactions: "I don't know what I hate about it the most." Someone else comments, "But we've been talking about it for an hour."

Soon other agencies, especially the upstarts, also began to be impious about products. Further uptown, the newly opened Wells Rich Greene, still housed in temporary space in the Gotham Hotel, tackled the advertising for a new, longer Philip Morris cigarette. Traditional advertising would have extolled its virtues in an expected way, but the WRG creative team called attention to the new length by making fun of it. The commercials talked about the *disadvantages* of Benson & Hedges. The cigarette could get mashed by closing elevator doors or entangled in someone's beard, all because it was "one silly little millimeter longer." Nobody had ever mutilated a brand that way before. Revolutionary! Destruction worked so well for Benson & Hedges that Wells Rich Greene did it again for American Motors. They had a crew of men with sledgehammers demolish a Ford Mustang to make way for the new American Motors Javelin.

The whole point of the copywriter–art director partnership was the creation of what David Ogilvy called the BIG IDEA. "Unless your advertising is based on a BIG IDEA," he told us time and time again, "it will pass like a ship in the night." There was no established procedure for getting to the idea. I've worked with lots of art directors, and the creative process is always different and often surprising. Sometimes the art director wrote the headline and I came up with the visual. Sometimes we'd talk about the assignment we were working on. We might read over the "strategy statement," the sacred scroll that gave us direction. The client and the agency worked together over weeks and often months to draw up this document. It told us who we were talking to—our target audience. It told us the most important message we had to communicate to the customer—the key consumer benefit or "promise" of the advertisement, and the RTB or "reason to believe" that the product really delivered the benefit.

Sometimes the art director and I would talk about anything *but* the assignment, just to get our minds started. And sometimes we would sit mutely for hours. The best art director I ever worked with, Doug, was one of the mute ones. He was a gentle Italian who wrote beautifully and came up with lots of BIG IDEAS. He was simply a man of few words when thinking up concepts. Let's say we were working on a new commercial for Dove soap. We'd sit for hours in my office not saying anything, just staring at each other or at the walls. One of us might say, "A dry riverbed." And the other might say, "A little complicated?" And then we'd sit and stare for a few more hours.

When my daughter Jenny was in third grade, she had to write a short description on the topic "What My Daddy Does All Day." Well, Jenny had visited my office too, and she was enough of an early feminist to reshape the topic into "What My Mommy Does All Day." She wrote, "My mommy stays in her office all day with a man and they look at the ceiling." A week later, I saw Jenny's teacher in the school hallway and she asked, "Mrs. Maas, exactly what *do* you do?"

David Ogilvy made his own special contributions to the creative revolution. One of them was what he called "story appeal." He wanted the visual in every print advertisement to make the reader lean forward and ask, "What's going on here?" David wrote in *Confessions of an Advertising Man* that one day when he was on his way to the photo shoot for one of the newest clients at his young agency some instinct made him stop at a drugstore and buy an eye patch. He convinced the model, George Wrangel, to put it on. The result was "The Man in the Hathaway Shirt." Mysterious, sexy, exotic, sophisticated advertising, it put Ogilvy & Mather on the map.

David also managed to popularize snob appeal. He turned Commander Whitehead, the red-bearded British head of the Schweppes company, into the spokesman for Schweppes tonic water. I remember one commercial that showed him arriving in America by ship. He strode down the gangplank while his Rolls-Royce and his product were unloaded simultaneously.

D.O. wrote one of the world's most famous headlines in an advertisement for Rolls-Royce. The visual was simply a sleek photo of the car. The headline said: "At 60 miles an hour, the loudest noise in this new Rolls-Royce comes from the electric clock." The chief engineer at Rolls-Royce, on seeing this ad, is said to have remarked, "Damn that clock. I knew it would give us trouble."

Ogilvy's most lasting gift to the advertising world was proving the importance of market research. His work with the Gallup research firm had convinced him that the more you knew about your consumers, the better your chances of persuading them to buy your brand. Today, Procter & Gamble freely admits that knowing their customer inside out is one of the two key reasons they are the leaders in virtually every category in which they compete. Product quality is the other reason.

In the sixties, the Ogilvy clients most interested in acquiring this kind of information were Lever Brothers and General Foods. Since their brands were purchased mostly by women, our agency became steeped in knowledge of "what women want." Focus groups were a popular form of consumer research. A research company would recruit six or eight women who normally purchased certain goods or services. They'd sit around a table for about two hours as a professional moderator led them in a discussion about their concerns and needs, likes and dislikes. Focus group discussion rooms always had one-way mirrors: people from the client company and people from the agency could sit in a dark room behind a mirrored wall and watch the proceedings. Our agency, with the help of focus groups, saved several clients from potential disaster.

THE CHEAP COFFEE CAPER

During an economic downturn, General Foods decided to bring out an inexpensive coffee, and my creative group was given the assignment. It was made with chicory for a robust flavor with fewer coffee beans, similar to Louisiana coffee—admittedly a polarizing taste. My team thought the coffee was awful, but we plunged ahead into the project.

The women in the focus groups didn't simply dislike the taste. They *loathed* it. Even worse, they were outraged by the whole idea behind the product. One woman summed up the general attitude: "I'll stop putting meat on my table before I'll serve my husband cheap coffee!" After the first few groups, I went up to General Foods headquarters in White Plains and told them the bad news. The men in the brand group refused to believe me, so I played them a few typical nuggets from the audiotapes. And that was the end of the cheap coffee. Poor little product. It never even got a name.

THE BATTER FRY FIASCO

Every so often, though, focus groups failed us. General Foods and Ogilvy made Shake 'n Bake a big success almost overnight. The product was just a bag and a flavored dry coating mix; the user simply put the chicken parts in the bag with the mix, shook, and baked. Voilà! Crispy fried chicken taste without the work of frying. Kids loved to help with the shaking part, and the agency developed a little dance we called "the Shake 'n Bake Shake."

Urged on by the win with Shake 'n Bake, the test kitchens at General Foods soon came up with a second fried chicken entry: a product that would make authentic Southern fried chicken, the kind with a batter coating similar to Colonel Sanders's Kentucky Fried Chicken. It came with the familiar paper bag and a dry mix to which you added water and, I think, an egg to make the batter. Then you put the chicken parts into the bag with the batter and . . . well, you couldn't shake; you had to sort of knead and massage.

We did tons of research. We took the concept into focus groups, where women told us they loved the idea of an easy way to get Southern fried chicken. And they loved the taste of the prepared chicken we served them. We took the finished product into taste tests, where it was a huge hit. Men loved it, kids loved it. Women clamored to buy the product. The agency named it Batter Fry.

General Foods decided to put the product into a few moderate-size cities as test markets. We needed to run advertising in these cities, of course, and General Foods approved a storyboard with a former Miss America from somewhere in the South. The script called for her to take a hearty bite from a Batter Fry leg, chew with gusto, and remark, "This is Southern fried chicken just like my momma used to make." When we filmed the commercial, we wanted to do ten or twelve takes as usual to make sure we had the perfect shot. After the second take, Miss America refused to eat another bite: she would get nauseous and, even worse, she would get fat. The lawyers agreed that as long as she had indeed eaten the product at least once, they were satisfied. For the rest of the filming, the actress took a big bite, and the camera cut away to a close-up of the crispy chicken while she daintily spit her mouthful into a bowl held by the prop man.

The test markets opened, the commercial ran, and Batter Fry flew out of food stores. Within two weeks, however, we knew something was terribly wrong: there were no repeat purchases. The team from the agency flew to the nearest market to interview some of the women who'd bought the product. They were furious. It turned out that they didn't have the expertise of the cooks in the General Foods kitchens and couldn't make the batter stick to the chicken. What it did do wonderfully was seep out of the bag onto kitchen counters and stovetops, where it adhered permanently. The women assured us that on all measures, Batter Fry outperformed Krazy Glue.

But that wasn't the worst of it. The deep-frying was a challenge to almost all of them. If the fat was not precisely the right temperature, once the determined cook managed to get the chicken into the pan, geysers of hot grease shot skyward and smoke poured from the pan and billowed to the ceiling. The smell was overwhelming. One woman cried as she told us about her experience. Another threatened to come to White Plains and punch the president of General Foods. "The bastard. He ruined my kitchen!"

We dried all the tears, settled the complaints, and quietly folded the test markets. Batter Fry joined the cheap coffee in the General Foods graveyard. The client and the agency made a vow that for all future food products, we would make sure the women not only tasted them but prepared them, too.

OGILVY VILLAGE

The creative revolution didn't change all advertising overnight. A lot of prerevolutionary activity continued. This was still the era of the mnemonic device, a visual effect like cups turning into percolators for Maxim coffee. There were lots of other popular effects. The White Knight rode through kitchens for Ajax; he pointed his spear at dirt or wax buildup and—pow!—it disappeared. One dishwashing liquid competed with Dove's white doves by creating a storm in our sinks: waves crashed, thunder rolled, and dishes arose cleansed from the deep. Every time anyone took a bite of Imperial margarine, its "fit for a king" taste made a huge crown pop up on his head.

It was also the era of the "continuing character." One creative director at Ogilvy imagined we could people an entire village. There was Cora, who ran the country store and refused to sell any coffee other than Maxwell House coffee. (Cora was portrayed by Margaret Hamilton, a gentle soul whose most famous role was the Wicked Witch of the West in the movie *The Wizard of Oz*.) In his store down the street, Pete the Butcher extolled the virtues of Shake 'n Bake, while in the town library, Marian the Librarian recommended Ex-Lax. Willie the Plumber drove his van through town rescuing housewives with Drano.

As a viewer, you always knew when a continuing character was appearing for the first time. The commercial would open with the storefront emblazoned with the name: "Cora's Country Store." Then you would hear a voice: "Welcome to Cora's Country Store." Then you would see the person: "Hi, I'm Cora."

Other agencies contributed to the town population. Among the best known were Madge the Manicurist for Palmolive dish soap; Rosie the Diner Owner for Bounty; the sad Maytag Repairman; and yet another plumber, Josephine, played by former child actress Jane Withers, for Comet scouring powder.

Scattered around the countryside were animated continuing characters: the Jolly Green Giant, the Pillsbury Doughboy, the Campbell's Kids, Elsie the Cow. Charlie the Tuna swam in the neighboring ocean, hoping to be caught but always thrown back as not good enough for StarKist.

By far the most famous, or infamous, continuing character of them all was Mr. Whipple, the store manager. He always pleaded with his customers not to squeeze the Charmin toilet paper, even though it was "irresistibly soft." But he never could resist squeezing it himself. Mr. Whipple squeezed Charmin for twenty-five years, and during that entire time it was the most detested and most successful advertising on television. Consumers loathed it because it banged away at them like the Anacin hammers, but they remembered the message and bought the product anyway.

The creative people at Benton & Bowles, the Charmin agency, grew heartily sick of the campaign, but they couldn't come up with any advertising that would beat its scores in the testing Procter & Gamble used. And P&G would never take successful advertising off the air unless they had something better. Copywriters grew palsied and gray trying to knock off Mr. Whipple. The story went around that one poor devil at B&B threatened to shoot him. Finally, after all those years, Procter relented and replaced the campaign with one that had tested *almost* as well. The actor who played George Whipple retired a fairly wealthy man. P&G sent him a case of Charmin every month for the rest of his life.

Another result of the creative revolution was "agency churn." Previously, client-agency partnerships were marriages that lasted for decades. Suddenly, clients saw consumers responding to the attention-getting advertising from Doyle Dane Bernbach and the new hot shops being opened by people like Mary Wells, George Lois, and Jerry Della Femina. Maybe one of those crazy new agencies could reinvigorate *their* brand. So they would fire the sleepy old agency that had been doing their ads for thirty years and award the business to one of the new places. The old agency, now in a panic to attract a replacement account, would hire a creative team from one of the hot shops. The new team would turn out work so foreign to the old agency's culture that their account men didn't have the stomach to present it. Often, the young creative whiz kids, aliens at the traditional agencies, would crawl back home and ask to be rehired. Often, the traditional brands, strangers to the revolutionary culture, would return to their old agencies. But over time, the Anacin school of advertising died out and the agencies who continued to practice it slowly faded away.

David Ogilvy liked to hire copywriters and art directors from different creative cultures. He would find out who was responsible for ads and commercials he liked, call them at their agencies, and ask them to come in for a chat. He saw an ad written by Gene Grayson, then a copywriter at Ted Bates, and called his office. Grayson answered. "This is David Ogilvy," Ogilvy announced. "And this is Abraham Lincoln," Grayson said, and hung up. Ogilvy called back. Grayson went to work for Ogilvy & Mather, stayed for many years, and laid the creative foundations that made Dove the world's bestselling soap.

David also persuaded George Lois, a young art director at DDB, to come in for an interview. Lois was turning out ads that shattered traditions left and right. Ogilvy offered him a big creative job at three times what Lois was making. George politely declined. Some fifty years later, talking with me, George recalled their conversation: "Mr. Ogilvy, it's impossible. You have 284,000 rules against the kind of advertising I do."

D.O. did manage to lure at least one prize from Doyle Dane Bernbach. Copywriter David Herzbrun came to the agency in 1965. Herzbrun was best known for his classic commercial for Volkswagen, which asked, "Have you ever wondered how the snowplow driver drives *to* the snowplow?" and revealed that the answer was in a VW. And for his commercial for the Broxident electric toothbrush, for which he coined the slogan "You brush with an ordinary toothbrush but you brrrrrrrrrrush with a Brrrrroxident." He was exactly the sort of fertile creative force David Ogilvy was looking for. Herzbrun lasted at Ogilvy & Mather for just two years, didn't get a single memorable ad approved, and went home to DDB.

Another revolution-inspired event was an increase in the kind of new business presentation that became known as a "shoot-out" or "bake-off." Some dozen agencies, often more, would be invited to present speculative creative work, for which they received no remuneration. The winning agency was awarded the business. Well, that approach didn't work, either, since the speculative advertising almost never was produced. The new agency didn't have the brand DNA yet running in their veins, the creative approaches weren't *quite* right, and the client got cold feet. Lots of clients came back, whimpering, and asked their original agencies to forgive and forget.

In the good old days, accounts were awarded more civilly, usually during a postprandial brandy in a men's club. David

Ogilvy tells of acquiring one of his early British accounts by means of a luncheon at the House of Commons. He sent the prospective client a note: "Mr. Ogilvy is dining with the secretary of state for Scotland. They would be pleased if you could join them."

Earlier, there was more room for generosity of spirit. Ogilvy was competing with the Grey agency for the Greyhound Bus account. On the way to the presentation, D.O. and the head of Grey showed each other their campaigns. Grey's was the famous "Take the bus. And leave the driving to us." Ogilvy told the Greyhound advertising manager that Grey deserved to win the account.

Earlier, agency leaders had the courage to turn down bullies. Another David Ogilvy example: the Rayon Association told him, "You will have exactly fifteen minutes to present your advertising. At that point, we will ring this bell." "Ring the bell," David said, and walked out. At Ogilvy & Mather, we used this as a mantra against mean clients. "Ring the bell," we'd mutter. We couldn't walk out, because it wasn't our agency, but we felt that if David knew the client was browbeating us, that is what he'd do. It stiffened our spines and raised our morale.

THE SLIPPERY PATH TO JOHNSON WAX

A senior account man at Ogilvy had a good friend who became head of marketing at the S. C. Johnson Company, makers of Johnson Wax and other household products. We were invited to make a new business presentation. David did not believe in speculative creative work, but he always encouraged us to do all the research we possibly could. It was midsummer, and Michael, the girls, and I were spending weekends at our tiny house in Westhampton Beach, so I used my neighbors as guinea pigs. I distributed dozens of cans of Johnson Wax and competing products to women all over town, asked them to do half their kitchen floors with one, half with another, and report on the results. We picked up some fresh insights that were made part of the new business pitch, and the account group asked me to present the findings.

The date was set for the meeting; it turned out to be right in the middle of my vacation. "I'm going to lose a whole day going back and forth to the city," I moaned to the senior account man in charge. "Don't worry. We'll send a seaplane for you." They did. Michael drove me to the appointed spot and, right on time, the plane landed in the bay and skied in fairly close to shore. The pilot, in Bermuda shorts, climbed out on a pontoon and waved at me. Cheerily, I waved back. Michael realized the problem. "He can't get any closer. It's too shallow. You'll have to wade out to him."

I was wearing an expensive new black silk pantsuit purchased just for the presentation. "Wade! It's practically up to my thighs." There was nothing I could do but roll the silk pants up as high as they'd go, carry my shoes in one hand and my pocketbook in the other, and hope I wouldn't slip on the oozy bay bottom. The pilot hauled me aboard, I waved to Michael, and away we flew. I was still slightly damp when I made the presentation. Damp and very wrinkled.

We won the Johnson business, and so began almost weekly trips to Racine, Wisconsin, where the Johnson headquarters is a landmark building designed by Frank Lloyd Wright. At our first meeting, "Mr. Sam" Johnson, representing the fourth generation of family ownership, showed us around. "We haven't changed one thing from the original Wright building," he told us proudly. "And we won't." At about four o'clock that afternoon, as our daylong meeting continued, it began to rain. All the Johnson people calmly put up umbrellas and continued the briefing. It turned out the old building leaked like a sieve. "We've been trying to solve this problem without sacrificing any architectural integrity," Mr. Sam said from beneath his umbrella. "So far, nothing has worked."

Another challenge of the building was the Wright-designed chairs. The executive chairs were solid enough, but the secretarial chairs had only three legs. They looked elegant but proved dangerously unsteady. A secretary had to keep both feet firmly planted on the floor; if she dared to cross her legs, the chair would pitch her backward, head over heels. It made for an unusual spectator sport.

THE *REAL* PATRICIA NEAL STORY

In 1986, I wrote my autobiography, *Adventures of an Advertising Woman.* Many books about advertising written by heads of agencies are really thinly disguised new business presentations. David Ogilvy admitted that his bestselling *Confessions of an Advertising Man* was just that. Jerry Della Femina, in *From Those Wonderful Folks . . .*, said that the advertising agency world wasn't really what people thought. "The wild stuff, I'm afraid, is very much overrated." In his preface to a new edition published forty years later, Jerry wrote that what actually went on in advertising agencies of the 1960s would make *Mad Men* look like *Rebecca of Sunnybrook Farm.* I asked him why he changed his story. "I was running an advertising agency back then, and clients were a conservative lot." Today, Jerry is still running an agency, but he knows clients now like to think creative people are all a little wild, like Don Draper. Maybe that gives them more confidence in us.

My *Adventures* was a whitewashed memoir. I was president of a New York advertising agency and thought the book would help to attract new business. So all the clients I described were smart and strategic, all our campaigns worked, and there was never a cloud in the blue sky over Madison Avenue. Nobody drank, smoked, or had adulterous sex. Nobody even had nonadulterous sex. My account of Patricia Neal and the Maxim coffee campaign was prettied up in a similar way. I didn't want General Foods, makers of Maxim, to appear foolish. More important, I loved Pat and didn't want to write a word that would be hurtful to her. Pat is dead now, so I can tell the whole story.

All the research we did with General Foods about American women and coffee suggested that the greatest compliment they could receive was having their husbands ask for a second cup. We decided to adopt that as the positioning for Maxim and immediately thought of enlisting Patricia Neal as our spokeswoman. Pat and her husband, writer Roald Dahl, were the world's favorite devoted couple. She was one of the most beautiful and talented actresses in Hollywood. He was a ruggedly handsome Norwegian, a former World War II RAF fighter pilot who also served with British Intelligence. Roald was one of the most popular and highest-paid authors in the English language, with books and films like *James and the Giant Peach* and *Charlie and the Chocolate Factory.*

"I didn't yet love Roald when we were married," Pat told me. "I was still deeply in love with Gary Cooper." Pat, just twenty-three years old, starred with Cooper in *The Fountainhead* in 1949. They had an affair that lasted several years, but Cooper was Catholic and would not divorce his wife. Pat wanted to settle down and start a family. She married Roald in 1953, had four children, continued her stage and screen career, and won the Academy Award as Best Actress for her role in *Hud* in 1964. A year later, pregnant with their fifth child, Pat suffered a massive stroke that left her partially paralyzed and unable to speak.

Roald devoted himself full-time to nursing, cajoling, and coercing her back to near normalcy. He made her walk; he made her talk. If she wanted something, she had to ask for it by name; otherwise she did without. "He badgered me," Pat recalled. "But he threw me back into deep water, which was exactly where I belonged." His treatment worked. Pat recovered almost completely, and the story of their devotion became famous. Who would be a better spokesperson for Maxim, the husband-pleasing coffee? General Foods sent a case of the coffee to the Dahl home in Great Missenden, England, both Pat and Roald tasted it and liked it, and we made her a handsome offer.

Roald turned it down. I knew from that first moment that he was going to be trouble, but I couldn't even have guessed how much. He asked for *twice* the amount General Foods offered; they accepted. He asked for first-class airfare when commercials would be filmed in the United States. That was standard, especially for a star like Patricia Neal; he demanded an *additional* first-class ticket for a companion. General Foods agreed to this, too. Finally, he asked for script approval. I begged GF not to give in to this, but they felt Pat would boost Maxim sales and didn't want to risk losing her. So Roald and I began a three-year sparring match.

For one script, I wanted Pat to talk about serving Maxim when "company comes for dinner." Roald scoffed at me over the telephone. "'Company' is such a middle-class word. It's so *American*." I responded, "So are the people drinking the coffee." I won that round, but Roald usually had the advantage. He had script approval, and he had Pat. In the second year of the campaign we got around him by filming *unscripted* commercials. I would stand out of camera range and throw questions at Pat; she'd ad-lib answers. With no lines to memorize, Pat was at her natural best in these spots, laughing her husky, sexy laugh. They were our most memorable TV spots.

We filmed the first two commercials in a London studio, but Roald suggested that from then on we film in New York. That seemed a strange request, simply because it meant tiring travel for Pat, but it made our own lives easier. We soon found out why Roald suggested this. General Foods would send the funds for two first-class tickets, and he would buy *one* economy-class ticket and put Pat on the plane alone. British Airways, those classy folks, always bumped her back up to first again.

When the Patricia Neal campaign had been running for over a year, and Maxim sales were up, Dahl sprang his most outrageous request: "Since Pat talks about me in every spot and how much I like your damn coffee, I am virtually appearing in your commercials, and should be compensated accordingly." So for several years General Foods paid Roald Dahl residuals for being an unseen presence in the advertising. It was a first.

The fallout of the Maxim campaign continued. As we prepared to film the first commercials in London, we hired a production company run by two young Englishwomen of distinguished background. They did a splendid job dressing the sets and collecting the props, right down to the perfect coffee cups. One of the two partners, Felicity Crosland, personally made a trip to the Dahl home with wardrobe for Pat. Roald did not like the selection, and Felicity went back and forth from London to Great Missenden three or four times before he was satisfied.

It turns out Dahl was more than satisfied. He and Felicity began an affair then and there. The Maxim campaign ran its course, but Pat and I remained friends. A few years later she called to tell me that Roald was divorcing her to marry Felicity. "And remember that it was *you* who brought them together."

David Ogilvy knew Roald Dahl; they had worked at British Intelligence together. I wrote to tell him about the divorce. "Poor Pat," he wrote back. "Roald is a shit."

CHAPTER 8

Sex in Advertising

There are two kinds of sex in advertising. The first kind uses sex appeal, including nudity and innuendo, to sell products. The second also aims to sell products, but relies on sexual stereotypes like the sweet little housewife or the big dumb husband. I confess I am guilty of the second kind.

It's not entirely my fault. For most of my career, I was writing advertising for brands that sold to women, brands that were generally meant to clean your house or feed your family. Most successful advertising mirrors society; it doesn't lead the way. In the world of the sixties, there was only one person doing the cleaning and the cooking. It was SHE. And the reason she was doing all that cleaning and cooking was to please HIM.

Take Dove-for-Dishes. Its positioning, its sole reason for being, was to keep a woman's hands soft and smooth despite all that dishwashing. So it follows that *women* had to man the sinks. I tried to sell Lever Brothers a campaign that featured *men* doing the dishes with Dove, and being mercilessly teased by their buddies because of their gorgeous hands. One commercial would have shown two burly construction workers with jackhammers. One notices his pal's hands and exclaims, "Your hands, Eddy. Look at your hands! Elizabeth Taylor should have those hands!"

My Lever clients thought it was a terrible idea, but they allowed me to turn it into a radio campaign we tested for a few weeks one summer. It didn't work. The radio commercials made people laugh, but they didn't sell any dishwashing liquid. So we went back to women at the sinks.

Maxim coffee is another example. It was launched on a positioning of "tastes like fresh-perked coffee," but when Taster's Choice appeared a year later with exactly the same strategy, General Foods decided to move to a different niche. Tons of research and dozens of focus groups suggested that women felt their coffee was perfect if their husband liked it. He didn't even have to praise it; he could just sit reading the morning paper and drinking it. If she offered him a second cup and he accepted with a grunt, she would stick with that coffee brand forever. So we moved to the "husband-pleasing strategy" and the Patricia Neal campaign. After Pat, we ran a series of commercials showing men engaged in some outdoor activity like fishing or sailing, coming home to be greeted by the wife and the Maxim.

All this copywriting had its consequences. The National Organization for Women awarded me its first ever NOW award for the "Most Obnoxious Commercial of the Year Depicting Women." It was for Dove, of course, for chaining all those women to sinks.

But NOW didn't stop there. A year later, we had a terrific

commercial running for Maxim. It showed a man and his son at the helm of a sailboat, spray flying, the wind riffling their hair. And where was good old Mom? Down in the dank galley, making the Maxim. Bingo! I won the NOW award a second time. As far as I know, I am the only copywriter to have been so recognized two years in a row.

Neither Maxim coffee nor Dove-for-Dishes is around today. I have always thought that our husband-pleasing strategy killed Maxim. As feminism came in, husband-pleasing went out. And ultimately Lever Brothers decided that a dishwashing liquid, even a gentle one, was too harsh a product for the Dove family of products, and they axed the bird.

I wasn't NOW's only target. At one point, they picketed Olivetti's New York showroom and railed at George Lois for depicting only *women* as secretaries in all his Olivetti typewriter commercials. Lois responded with a spot that cast Jets quarterback Joe Namath, *the* macho man of the era, as a secretary. (Namath really did know how to type.) At the end of the spot, the boss (a woman) comes out of her office and says, "You do very good work, Joseph. By the way, what are you doing for dinner tonight?"

The National Organization for Women must have despised most of the advertising created in the 1960s to sell products to women. At Ogilvy & Mather we had lots of these brands, with slogans that NOW surely found demeaning, like "the Maxwell Housewife." Even our headline for Aim, an anticavity toothpaste, targeted women, not men: "Great news for mothers of cavity-prone children."

In our advertising for Shake 'n Bake, Roast 'n Boast (a gravy product), and Good Seasons salad dressing, it was clear who was doing the shaking, the roasting, and the seasoning. The only food preparation that featured a man was for Open Pit barbecue sauce, and even there, a woman played a supporting role. The husband barked, "Where's the Open Pit?" and the wife came running across the grass with the product in her hand and fell into it. You never saw a woman in those early Ogilvy commercials drive a Mercedes, pay with an American Express card, drink Puerto Rican rum, or expound on the benefits of Owens Corning fiberglass insulation or Toro lawn mowers.

Peggy Olson could have been a copywriter at Ogilvy. She always studies the product, reads all the research, learns about the consumer's needs and desires, and comes up with a concept for the advertising. Today we would call it a "consumer insight" that contributes to the "brand architecture." Back then, it was just called an idea.

I often sympathize with Peggy when she is working on a product for women and runs into opposition from men, at both the agency and with the client, who think they know women better than she does. The Pepsi client insists on launching Patio diet cola with a commercial imitating Ann-Margret singing "Bye Bye Birdie." Peggy tries to persuade Don that this is a product aimed at women who want to lose weight, and a sexy woman is not the way to appeal to them. Don pooh-poohs her. "Men want her; women want to look like her," he says. Peggy is vindicated when the commercial is a flop.

The failure of the Ann-Margret look-alike reminded me of how hard it is to predict whether or not a celebrity is going to succeed as pitchman for a particular brand. Patricia Neal was such a natural choice for Maxim that we didn't even bother to do any research about her. I wasn't so lucky with another celebrity suggestion to General Foods, this time for Good Seasons salad dressing. The Italian flavor was far and away the most popular, so the client was looking for an appropriate spokeswoman. I discovered that actress Sophia Loren had just written an Italian cookbook and suggested that she would be perfect. My creative director loved the idea; so did the account men at the agency, and so did the client. Just to be on the safe side, we did some focus group testing. "Sophia Loren?" the women scoffed. "Sophia Loren! She couldn't find her way to the kitchen with a map!"

I moved off Good Seasons, so their eventual choice of celebrity took me completely by surprise. They tapped Anna Maria Alberghetti, a petite and pretty Italian singer probably best remembered for her Tony-winning performance as Lili in the Broadway musical *Carnival*, and as Maria in *West Side Story*. I am told she sold a lot of salad dressing.

The network censors and the Federal Communications Commission began to get tougher about brand endorsements. The celebrities really had to use the products, and be willing to sign affidavits to attest to the fact. There was a difference between appearing in a dramatization as an actor and doing an endorsement. When Jane Withers was Josephine the Plumber for Comet cleanser, she didn't need to use Comet or even like it. If she had appeared as herself, that would have been a different matter. The rules became even more stringent, and any endorser had to use the product for six months before they were able to appear in a commercial for it.

But what network censor could look into the hearts of men or spokesmen and know the truth? Many celebrities may have fibbed a bit in order to land lucrative contracts. I'm told that one well-known Hollywood star, a little down on his luck, heard that a particular brand—let's call it Early Spring—was looking for a spokesperson. He called the casting director and swore up and down that he had been using Early Spring faithfully for two years. Nobody had told him it was a vaginal deodorant.

If you have ever been on the set for a commercial shoot, you probably wondered why so many people are necessary to make a piece of film that lasts only thirty seconds—sometimes only fifteen seconds. Well, a lot of them are there to make sure the talent looks just right and acts just so. There's "hair and makeup," sometimes one person, but often two different specialists, particularly for a beauty product. There's the costume designer, who makes such weighty decisions as whether the housewife scrubbing the floor should wear a dress or a skirt and a blouse. To give the director a wide selection, the designer will usually bring twenty or thirty choices to the set, with two of everything in case something gets stained. The designer doesn't help the talent get dressed or undressed, though; that's up to the wardrobe mistress, who also sees to the ironing, if it's necessary. To make sure the talent knows the lines, and says them just fast enough or slow enough to fill the thirty seconds, somebody rehearses the actors against a stopwatch. When I was involved in the filming of commercials, this job was officially titled "script girl" even if done by a man. Just as the electrician's assistant was called "best boy," even if a woman had the job. Today, gender neutrality has come to commercial production. The script girl is now a "script supervisor" and the best boy has dwindled into just an "assistant."

The time and trouble we took with the talent was nothing compared to how much we fussed with the products to make them look their best. Or better than their best. In those early days of television production, it was okay to "pretty up" the product. If your whipped cream melted under the hot lights, you could substitute shaving cream, which looked the same but held its peaks. If some of the famous Maxim coffee nuggets had turned to powder in the jar, we would carefully sift the coffee, find the perfect nuggets, and put them back on top of the jar, where the camera could zoom in for a close-up.

Nobody paid much attention to such glamorizing until the infamous "marbles in the soup" commercial for Campbell's soup. Actually, in this case neither the advertising agency nor the film production company was falsifying anything; it was simply a problem because the vegetables all sank to the bottom of the bowl and disappeared from view. They put marbles in the soup to prop up the vegetables that indeed were there. But some network censor cried foul and suddenly it became a cause célèbre. Consumers then decided that all television demonstrations were rigged; letters to the editor inveighed against advertising instead of politics; the advertising industry was in crisis. All over a couple of innocent marbles.

Then we were hit with yet another set of regulations about "product beautification." If you were making a coffee commercial, and the whipped cream was merely an unimportant prop, you could substitute shaving cream. But when you were making a *whipped cream* commercial, you had to use the real thing. If it melted under the lights, that was your problem. If your leading lady showed up with a blotchy complexion the morning of the shoot, it was permissible to cover the blotches with makeup *unless* the product was germane to a clear complexion, like a moisturizing soap or an anti-acne cream. In that case, you had to wait for the blotches to clear. Or find yourself another actress. These regulations haven't eased. Today, both the film production company and the agency producer have to sign a legal affidavit declaring the product has not been enhanced or tampered with in any way.

The sixties had definite regulations about film production but were a little schizophrenic about sex. We talked a lot about sex, the Pill, the Kinsey Report, Masters and Johnson, and women's newfound sexual freedom. But young women were still expected to enter marriage as virgins. Even if they did engage in premarital sex, they were not supposed to talk about it. In 1962, Helen Gurley Brown published *Sex and the Single Girl* and shocked us all. The very title was an oxymoron. I first met Helen when, as the new editor in chief of *Cosmopolitan* magazine, she spoke at a huge New York advertising conference in 1964. Somebody couldn't attend the lunch at the last minute, so I—the newest, most wet-behind-the ears copywriter at Ogilvy—was given the ticket. The Grand Ballroom of the Waldorf was packed to the balconies. Helen arose with the dessert and talked. In passing, she mentioned two advertising trends of the day as she saw them: sex and sincerity. She finished her talk and asked for questions from the audience. There were none. So I, always the cheerleader, stood up, found a microphone, introduced myself, and asked how she managed to link sex and sincerity. "Why, Jane Maas," she lectured me, "don't you know that the best kind of sex is sincere?" The audience applauded; I blushed and sat down.

Helen and I became friends. In the mid-1980s, she was at the height of her *Cosmo* fame; I was president of Muller Jordan Weiss, a medium-sized New York advertising agency, and eager to attract new clients. Radio and TV talk show hosts began to invite me to take the "against" position in discussions about the increasing sexuality of advertising. (I guess I had a sort of clean-scrubbed aura.) Actually, I could have taken either side, but I thought the buzz would be good for new business. Helen and I were once pitted against each other on one of the network morning shows to debate the Calvin Klein print ads for Obsession cologne, which featured intertwined nude male and female bodies. Helen defended the ads; I think Obsession was a *Cosmopolitan* advertiser. "They just seem like happy little puppies," she said. "I wouldn't want young children to see these puppies," I objected. Helen took a deep breath. "I wouldn't, either," she agreed. Nifty lady.

I did some consulting work with her during her long and super-successful tenure at *Cosmopolitan*. I still think of her often because I follow the most important piece of advice she ever gave me, in *Sex and the Single Girl:* never undertip. It's not sexy.

Meanwhile, creative people at many agencies were cashing in on the sexually charged atmosphere of the era. Airlines, appealing primarily to male business travelers, began more and more to use attractive stewardesses as a come-on. I've already talked about Wells Rich Greene's "Air Strip" spot for Braniff.

You can view it now on YouTube and see for yourself what a sweetly innocent spot it is.

The airline advertising scandal of the sixties was caused by United Airlines, but only indirectly because of the advertising. United came up with a special promotion offering men a discounted airfare and hotel room if they took their wives along on a business trip. The commercials were fairly expected: scantily dressed wives dancing in a chorus line and singing pleadingly, "Take me along with you if you love me." United was so pleased with the results of this campaign that it followed up with a mailing to all the wives thanking them and hoping they enjoyed the trip. It turned out that a fair percentage of the wives who received these letters were quite surprised;

Jane Maas and co-author Ken Roman in their Ogilvy photo for the publication of *How to Advertise* in 1976.

they were not the ladies who had been along for the ride. United quietly folded the campaign.

It took National, with its 1971 "Fly Me" campaign, to create a backlash by women. The commercials featured sexy actresses dressed as National stewardesses looking directly at the camera and saying, "I'm Cheryl." (Or Nancy, Margie, or Barbara.) "Fly me." The airlines painted the women's names on the noses of the planes in the style of World War II bombers, and passed out "Fly me" buttons for the hostesses to wear. Some of them refused. Others urged the Federal Communications Commission to take the campaign off the air. NOW thundered. And National passengers increased by 23 percent, twice that of any other airline.

In 1966, everybody was talking about the suggestive spot for Noxzema shaving cream. A man shaved to striptease music while a sexy female urged, "Take it off. Take it *all* off." The commercial ended with a kind of "bump and grind" musical riff as the shaver flicked off the last dabs of Noxzema the way a stripper would shed her last bits of clothing.

Another Noxzema spot, also for shaving cream, caused an even greater stir. It opened with a close-up of Joe Namath saying, "I'm so excited. I'm going to get creamed." Farrah Fawcett-Majors then smoothed on the Noxzema. Namath, cuddling with her at the end of the commercial, confided, "You've got a great pair of hands." Racy stuff.

The sexiest, most notorious commercial of the decade was written by a woman, Lois Geraci Ernst, founder of an agency called Advertising to Women. She created the "Aviance Night" for Aviance perfume, and struck right at the heart of Betty Friedan's "problem that has no name." The Aviance commercial shows the sweet little housewife changing from her floor-scrubbing garb into a negligee and spraying herself all over with Aviance. The music and lyrics that accompanied this scene were "I've been sweet and I've been good, I've had a whole day of motherhood, but I'm going to have an Aviance night." The newly seductive haus frau stations herself at the front door, her husband enters, BLACKOUT.

Print advertising was more lenient than television about sex. The network watchdogs would allow a slightly suggestive commercial like the striptease shave, but they drew the line at true sexual innuendo. Nudity was unheard of. You couldn't even show a woman wearing a bra. The famous "I dreamed I (DID WHATEVER) in my Maidenform bra" was a print campaign that ran from 1949 to 1969. The ads, showing women wearing only a bra above the waist, invited women to fantasize all kinds of activities, from attending the opera to going on a tiger hunt.

It wasn't until 1987 that television allowed a woman to appear in a bra. Previously, the bra makers had to parade their wares on a mannequin or on a model wearing the bra over a leotard.

The irrepressible George Lois, one of the 1960s bad boys in the agency business, created many covers for *Esquire* while he was a consultant to the magazine. One of his most controversial was for an issue themed "The New American Woman—through at 21." The cover photo Lois created was a nude young beauty dumped into a trash can. In his book *The Big Idea,* Lois confesses that his inspiration for this visual came from an old dirty joke. A young housewife is hanging her laundry on the rooftop of her apartment building. She trips and falls headfirst into a garbage can below. A Chinese laundryman passes by, admires her legs and nether parts, and says to himself, "Americans very funny people. In China, good for ten years yet."

George told me recently that the idea for one of his wittiest covers came from his wife. She was walking down Broadway a few weeks before the premiere of *Cleopatra,* the movie that had riveted the attention of the world because of the Elizabeth Taylor–Richard Burton love affair. Mrs. Lois knew that George was working on a cover idea for an upcoming *Esquire* piece on the movie. When she spotted two billboard painters working on an enormous Times Square poster of the lovers, she immediately called George. "Get down here right away. It's your cover photo!" He did, and knew he had his cover shot. The painters had just begun work on Taylor's breasts, each one nearly as large as the man painting it.

Lois came back the next day with a photographer. The painters had moved on past the breasts, but he gave them twenty dollars each to, as he says, "revisit the tits." It was another memorable George Lois cover.

Ogilvy & Mather in the 1960s was not a big proponent of sex in advertising. The most daring campaign we created was for Ban deodorant. We used semi-nude Greek statues as a way of showing armpits without showing armpits. The camera revolved around the statues while a "voice of God" announcer revealed solemnly that "in the adult male and in the adult female," there are certain glands that secrete sweat. Ban was the solution to these marmoreal outpourings. All of us at the agency were really proud of what we considered avant-garde advertising.

When sex did come to Ogilvy, it came with a bang. The cause was a series of print ads so sexy that they turned the agency into warring factions. It took David Ogilvy himself to make peace.

The first Ogilvy print ad for Paco Rabanne men's cologne showed a man in bed, clearly nude beneath sheets that just reached his hips. Morning light fills the room; an empty wine bottle stands on a chest at the foot of the bed. He is just answering the telephone. There is no headline and the copy is entirely a dialogue between the man and his lover of the night before.

> Hello?
> *You snore.*
> And you steal all the covers. What
> time did you leave?
> *Six-thirty. You looked like a*
> *toppled Greek statue lying there.*
> *Only some tourist had swiped*
> *your fig leaf.*

The lover says she (we assume she is a she, although some advertising critics believe the copywriter leaves this intentionally ambiguous) has taken his Paco Rabanne cologne. She is going to rub it on her body when she goes to bed and remember every little thing about their night together. The dialogue ends as her flight is called, and she asks what she should bring him from California. "My Paco Rabanne," he says. "And a fig leaf."

The new president of Ogilvy & Mather, Ken Roman, thought the ad was not in keeping with the agency's image. Chairman Jock Elliott agreed with him. They took the matter to the newly installed executive creative director, who reminded them that he had been promised complete creative freedom. The battle escalated to Touffou, where David Ogilvy was living in semi-retirement. He didn't like the ad, either, but he was chiefly offended by the fact that it had no headline, and therefore broke one of his most cherished rules: "Put the message in the headline." But even D.O. honored the "hands off the creative" commitment to the creative head.

There were several more ads in the series. Each one featured an evocative photo, erotic dialogue, and a missing bottle of the cologne. None of them had headlines. The campaign won the first Kelly Award from the Magazine Publishers Association for best print advertising of the year. More important, it created renewed buzz for Ogilvy & Mather as an exciting, creative advertising agency.

A year or so later, the creative director of the campaign, Jay Jasper, ran into David Ogilvy at the agency's Paris office. David confessed that he was using the Paco Rabanne ads in his new book *Ogilvy on Advertising* as an example of creative brilliance. He said, "You know, Jay, I'm eating a lot of crow in my book because of your campaign." The elevator doors opened and Ogilvy got on, just as Jasper said, *"Bon appétit,* David." Ogilvy smiled and the elevator doors closed.

In our book *How to Advertise,* first published in 1976 and still in print, Ken Roman and I offer some guidelines about the use of sex in advertising. "Sex may make the world go round," we say, "but it doesn't sell many products." We advise that sex works to sell sexy products, but not much else. We've been proved dead wrong. Sex has sold and continues to sell every product imaginable, from trucks to chewing gum.

It's my turn to eat crow.

CHAPTER 9

Why I Love New York

"I Love New York" is one of the most famous advertising campaigns in history and without question the most successful tourism promotion ever launched. Advertising people are always quick to claim credit; if we have contributed a comma, we claim a chapter. As a marketing consultant, I see lots of résumés from advertising people, and it surprises me how many of them say, flat out, "Creator of 'I Love New York.'" Sometimes the writer is more modest and claims only to have "played a pivotal role" in the advertising.

Success has many fathers, and there are a lot of men walking around New York State today who will look you in the eye and tell you they are the father of "I Love New York." The late governor Hugh Carey remembers saying, "I want people to love New York as much as I do." Genius copywriter Charlie Moss, working with art and film director Stan Dragoti, came up with the advertising campaign and the slogan. Another genius, designer Milton Glaser, gave us perhaps the best-known and most copied logo in the world. And yet one more monumental talent, Steve Karmen, wrote the song. Even publicist Bobby Zarem, whom *Time* magazine christened "Mr. Flack," says the campaign was his idea. Yes, all of these men are the fathers. But I can look you straight in the eye and tell you that I am its only mother. Mary Wells Lawrence was the godmother, of course, but I was the one who hugged it, fed it, and changed its diapers.

The tourism campaign had so many constituencies demanding attention and so many warring factions that somebody needed to be ringmaster and peacemaker. It turned out to be me. I was the liaison between the agency and the governor, the Department of Commerce, the state legislature, the regional tourism offices, the League of New York Theaters, the Statue of Liberty, the Baseball Hall of Fame, the Rockettes, the White House, and the Olympic Committee, to mention just a handful of my charges. The Adirondacks and Chautauqua both want to sponsor the official Fall Festival? Better send Jane to Plattsburgh to negotiate. The Finger Lakes wineries say the Long Island vineyards are upstarts? Jane needs to go to Ithaca. Oh, and better tell her to drop in at Jamesport, too. I have traversed almost every inch of this maddening, magical state. The Republicans think the Democrats are using "I Love New York" for their own ends? Jane better go to Albany. Again? Yes, again.

But back to the birth of the campaign. "Ford to New York: 'DROP DEAD.'" That was the headline in the *Daily News* in late 1975 when both the state and the city were nearly bankrupt and turned to the federal government for help. President Jerry Ford flatly refused. A lot of smart people put their heads together, including newly elected governor Hugh Carey, newly elected mayor Ed Koch, financial whiz Felix Rohaytyn, and commissioner of commerce John Dyson. One of the decisions they made was to reinvigorate tourism, which in the past had been the state's second-largest source of revenue. The Department of Commerce wisely decided they needed to hire an advertising agency, and they came to Wells Rich Greene. If you think of New York as a product, like a bar of soap, it was a daunting proposition. Even the client had to admit there were a few problems with the brand: people considered it dirty, difficult to use, expensive, and downright dangerous. Many agencies would turn down an assignment like that, but we accepted the challenge.

Our first job was to convince our clients not to spend a penny as yet on advertising, but to devote their entire tiny budget to research. We needed to find out why tourists came to New York and, even more important, why they didn't come. The research findings were astounding and the bedrock that supported the whole campaign. We discovered that New York State and New York City were two totally different products that appealed to two very different audiences. Traditionally they had been advertised together, a major marketing blunder. The *state* attracted the kind of all-American family who put the kids and the dog in the car and went off on a two-week summer vacation; the big lures for this audience were beaches, lakes, mountains, and outdoor recreation. The *city* beckoned to an older, more educated, more affluent "culture buff." One city feature stood head and shoulders above all others for attracting tourists the first time and drawing them back over and over again: Broadway theater. The research also told us that nobody thought of the state as a vacation destination—not even people living right here—a problem that advertising people call "low top of mind awareness." No wonder. New York's marketing budget for tourism was, per capita, the lowest of the fifty states. The agency and the Department of Commerce put together a massive presentation to persuade the state legislators that tourism was potentially a big moneymaker. It took several months of hemming and hawing, but finally, on April 1, 1977, they voted to invest $4.3 million in an advertising campaign.

The agency was under the gun to get advertising on television. People plan their summer vacations *months* in advance, so in order to make any impact at all on summer travel, we needed to have commercials on air no later than late May. That meant the creation of a new campaign, approvals by the state, casting, filming, editing—all in seven weeks. The normal schedule would require about four months. Enter Charlie Moss, responsible for some of the most memorable advertising campaigns ever, including "The end of the plain plane" for Braniff, "Flick your Bic," and "Midasize it." Charlie and Stan Dragoti dreamed up a thirty-second commercial that showed people from other states enjoying a New York vacation. A fisherman said, "I'm from New Hampshire but I love New York." A swimmer: "I'm from Cape Cod, but I love New York." The final vignette was a camper who declared, "I'm from Brooklyn, but I *looove* New York." The tagline for the spot was "If you love the outdoors, you'll love New York."

Then the magic started to happen. Every once in a great while, all the elements of an advertising campaign come together perfectly and the end result is greater than the sum of its parts. Music man Steve Karmen, known as "the king of the jingle jungle," looked at the film footage and went away to meditate. He could easily have stayed with the tagline and written a lyric celebrating "the outdoor state." Instead, he wrote "I Love New York." (It is now the official song of the state of New York, and was temporarily number two on the Japanese Hit Parade.) Designer Milton Glaser also picked up on "I Love New York" and created the great heart logo. The Department of Commerce wanted the logo to be in the public domain so every tourism attraction, large or small, could use it without charge. Dear, gentle Milton accepted a onetime fee of one thousand dollars for his design. It is worth untold millions. Maybe more.

The commercial began airing just before Memorial Day. To make up for the delay, we increased the frequency and used a technique called "roadblocking." This was still an era dominated by CBS, NBC, and ABC, so it was easy to ensure that anyone who watched the evening news on any channel would see our spot. We relearned an old lesson that those early "mad men" with the pounding hammers for Anacin already knew: repetition works. The response was immediate. Overnight, gas stations reported that they were out of New York State maps. And New York City cabdrivers, a notoriously cynical lot, blossomed forth with "I Love New York" bumper stickers. The research we conducted at the end of the summer said that 90 percent of the people in our target markets were aware of the advertising. Not bad, when you consider that only 89 percent of people in the United States know that Christopher Columbus discovered this country.

Jane confers with New York governor Hugh Carey during the "I Love New York" campaign.

Jane with Governor Hugh Carey and New York City mayor Ed Koch during the 1977 launch of "I Love New York."

Next it was time to focus on the other half of the "I Love New York" campaign: promoting tourism to the *city.* We knew from the earlier research that Broadway theater was the lure. That research also warned us that most visitors were concerned about "big-city hassle"—the expense and difficulty of buying theater tickets and finding a hotel room. So we created theater packages that included not only theater and hotel, but meals, sightseeing, even transportation. Charlie Moss and Stan Dragoti created a storyboard that featured the casts from current Broadway hits, all singing "I Love New York." Most of the theatrical producers were pleased to be part of the commercial, and the performers cheerfully went along with the decision. The only holdout was Yul Brynner, then starring in *The King and I.* We thanked his agent politely and said we had more than enough shows. Brynner soon realized he would be the only major star on Broadway *not* appearing in the commercial, and changed his mind.

It was a star-studded thirty seconds. In addition to the cast of *The King and I,* we had the casts of *A Chorus Line, Annie, Grease,* and *The Wiz,* plus Hume Cronyn and Jessica Tandy. Frank Langella as Dracula ended the commercial with the words "I love New York . . . especially in the evening." Then he turned away from the camera with a swirl of his black cloak. The commercial began to air on Valentine's Day and we did our usual "roadblocking" and then some. You couldn't turn on a television set without seeing our spot. The next day, long lines of people queued up for tickets of the shows we featured, the networks all sent out their television crews to cover this phenomenon, and Frank Langella became a matinee idol overnight. The impact on the city's economy was immediate, too: people came to see the shows, stayed in the hotels, ate in the restaurants, rode in the taxis. And the commercial went on to become the only one in history to win a Tony Award. Broadway loved New York very much.

Advertising that gets a lot of attention usually attracts its share of criticism, and it wasn't always smooth sailing my next year on the New York account. Wells Rich Greene was also creating ads for the state's economic development program, aimed at persuading businesses to move to New York. We wanted to humanize the department by putting a "face" on it, and the face we chose was that of the commissioner of commerce, John Dyson. When we ran his photo in a print ad, some members of the state legislature bristled, feeling John might be using this publicity to pave the way for public office. A special hearing was held in Albany to discuss deleting the photo from the advertisement. John, a man known more for his wit than his humility, showed up to protest the issue wearing a Lone Ranger mask. It made headlines all over the state and all over the country.

The vice chairman of Wells Rich Greene, who was also our comptroller, attorney, and general holy terror, cautioned everybody working on the New York account to be careful of every move we made. The Republicans were looking for mistakes, and the press was looking for stories. Almost immediately, I caused the next crisis. An art director and I had just completed an ad about the joys of camping in the state's mountains. We didn't have time to take a new photograph so had purchased a stock photo. The art director convinced me that the lake in the foreground looked kind of green; he wanted to retouch it and make it clear and blue. I agreed. The ad ran.

Some enterprising reporter who knew the area spotted our blunder. We had created a lake where none existed; the green area in the photo was actually a meadow. The reporter christened it "Lake Dyson," and tried to reach Mary Lawrence for comment. When he couldn't reach her, he called the vice chairman, who then called me at home just before midnight and roared at me so loudly that he woke Michael. Michael listened for about ten seconds, then grabbed the telephone from my hand. "I don't know who you are or why you're calling at this hour," Michael said, "but nobody shouts at my wife that way." Michael and the vice chairman became friends, and he never shouted at me again.

Then, too, there were my endless skirmishes with Audit & Control, the people who reviewed the agency invoices and paid our bills. The first tussle was over a print ad encouraging people to come and enjoy the state's fall foliage; a color photo proved it was indeed as spectacular as any in Vermont. Audit & Control informed me that payment for production of the ad was held up until they received a suitable explanation. They asked why it was necessary to spend so much extra money to do this ad in *color.* I simply sighed and went to Albany, armed with a copy of David Ogilvy's book, with a paper clip on the page about "story appeal in illustrations."

I was spending a lot of time in Albany, and a lot of it in meetings with Governor Carey and his staff. The brilliant, popular, charismatic Carey was already being mentioned in the press as a presidential candidate. Gradually, the governor began to confide in me. A widower, he worried about his twelve children, especially the younger ones, growing up in that rambling Albany mansion without a mother. Hugh Carey was also terribly lonely, and I think having that boisterous, exuberant, noisy brood of his around all the time sometimes made his loneliness even sharper. So I shouldn't have been surprised when he fell in love with Engie.

They met in Washington, at Ronald Reagan's inauguration in January 1980. Evangeline Gouletas was from a middle-class Greek family who came to the States in the 1950s and settled in Chicago. She and her two brothers, Nick and Vic, founded a real estate business, became millionaires, and never looked back. Engie was widowed, a young grandmother in her forties, exotic, sexy, and sleek; she always wore a gardenia in her black hair. The governor fell hard. He mounted a campaign that would have swept any woman off her feet, and I think this particular woman very much wanted to be swept. She began to visit New York City more and more often. Hugh Carey had met Michael by then, and we two couples began to double-date. As the romance progressed, the governor and I became even closer buddies. He often called me at Wells Rich Greene the day after one of our dinners together to get my progress report on the courtship. Most often, I would be sitting in a conference room filled with people working on "I Love New York." Writers, art directors, researchers, and account managers from the advertising agency and deputy commissioners of commerce and their staff members from New York State Tourism and Economic Development would all be there. The telephone in the center of the big table would ring, and someone would pick it up and announce, "Governor Carey calling Jane Maas." The room always fell silent.

"I think Engie had a good time last evening, don't you?" the governor would ask.

"I certainly do, sir," I would reply emphatically.

All eyes in the room were always on me. Were we discussing the state budget? The next election?

"Any suggestions about next steps?" he would continue.

"Well, sir, that needs a little strategic thinking on both our parts."

I loved every minute of it.

In March, Michael and I flew to Chicago to be with the governor and Engie to celebrate her name day (the feast day of the saint after whom you are named; to the Greeks a festive occasion far more important than a birthday). Hugh Carey gave her a ring that was almost identical to the one Prince Charles had recently given to Lady Diana. Although both the governor and Engie declared it a "friendship ring," those of us close to them guessed it was something more.

One Sunday in late March, the governor invited Michael and me to meet with him and Engie at her New York pied-à-terre for a "serious talk." I had a hunch they might be planning a fall wedding, possibly even a summer one. Their news was indeed the fact that they had decided to be married. After we all hugged and kissed and congratulated, Engie turned to me. "Hugh and I don't want a commercial wedding planner. We want someone who is close to us, someone we love, to run the wedding. Jane, will you do this for us?"

I panicked. Because I was Protestant and Michael was a Roman Catholic, our 1957 wedding was so small it was virtually an elopement. We were married by Father George Ford, a liberal priest who was considered rather a renegade at the time, but even he had to be discreet. So we had only two other people at our ceremony: Michael's parents, both Catholics. I didn't convert to Catholicism until ten years later, in the glow of dear old Pope John XXIII and all the new warmth and welcome of the church. When people asked me why I converted, I would say flippantly that just in case there really was a separate heaven for Catholics, I didn't want Michael over in that one with some blonde. But the real reason was that I was sharing everything else in life with Michael, and I wanted to share his religion, too.

But big weddings were a mystery to me. "I've never run a wedding," I stammered.

"I think you can't refuse," Michael said quietly. I knew he was right.

"If you really want me to, of course I will. And I am touched that you've asked me. What's the date?"

"My birthday," the governor said. "April eleventh. Two weeks from yesterday."

It didn't hit me until a few hours later. We had only twelve days to prepare for all the pomp and circumstance of a state wedding. The first thing I did the next day was to ask Mary Wells Lawrence for a two-week leave of absence without pay. I couldn't put the state of New York or my advertising agency in the compromising position of paying me while I ran a private function. My next call was to my friend Letitia Baldrige, to ask for advice on the many protocols of handling a wedding of this magnitude, with many guests who would need special treatment. Tish was the last word on etiquette. She had been Jackie Kennedy's chief of staff at the White House, where she was known as "General Baldrige." More recently she had written *The Amy Vanderbilt Complete Book of Etiquette.* If anyone would know all the answers, it would be Tish. She and

I had met a few years earlier when we were both winners of the coveted Matrix Award from Women in Communications, Tish for public relations, I for advertising.

She was wonderfully calm. "Helping you plan the wedding will be my wedding present to the bride and groom," she told me. "Now, the first thing to do is order the invitations from Tiffany's. Engraving will take about two weeks and calligraphy for addressing the envelopes another five days. I wonder if we should use the gubernatorial seal on the invitation?" she mused to herself. "Oh, yes, I think we should. When is the wedding to be?"

"A week from Saturday," I said.

Tish reeled. "What are we going to do about invitations?"

I had already discussed this issue with the bride-to-be and knew the dreaded answer. "We're going to send Mailgrams." Mailgrams were a cheaper form of Western Union telegrams, a sort of bulk mail device. Today's equivalent would be e-mailed wedding invitations.

Tish was stricken, but recovered. "Well, sometimes the finer points of etiquette must bow to larger concerns. But there are some dictates we absolutely must follow. The governor is a widower; Mrs. Gouletas is a widow. Since this is a second marriage for both of them, the wedding ceremony *must* be small. Only one attendant for each. Immediate family only."

I passed this information along to Engie, who smiled a small, quiet smile. "With one Greek family and one Irish family, the immediate family becomes very, very large. Probably in the hundreds." She also told me that in addition to her daughter, who was to be maid of honor, all five of the governor's daughters would be bridesmaids and all seven of his sons ushers.

Her tiny granddaughter, also an Engie, would be flower girl. Tish, hearing this and shuddering, told me seriously that she would have to withdraw from any official participation in the wedding. "I won't let you down, Jane. I won't leave you in the lurch. But I can't have my name associated with it."

Tish did hang in there as my adviser, bless her, wrinkling her patrician nose at almost every gaffe. She suggested that we have an engagement photo taken, and helped us book the famous fashion photographer Horst. Engie, Tish, and I were at his studio awaiting the arrival of the groom when we heard the sound of sirens. "Here comes Hugh," Engie announced.

Tish clapped her hands. "How wonderful to know that your true love cometh when you hear the sound not of trumpets, but of police sirens." The governor arrived, looking tense. I realized that Engie looked upset, as well. In fact, they both looked so haggard in the Horst photos that we never used them. After the photo shoot, I learned what had happened. Although Engie was "officially" a widow, she had in fact been married and divorced three times. On the marriage license, she swore to ex-husbands two and three, but somehow could not bear to acknowledge ex number one, and declared him dead. Of course, he popped up in the media the very next day, alive and well and living in California. The city clerk, future New York City mayor David Dinkins, had to return with a new marriage license to be signed. The New York district attorney, another future mayor named Rudy Giuliani, said he would not prosecute Engie for lying on the first license. At this point, all over the state, cars began to sport bumper stickers that proclaimed: "Honk if you've been married to Engie."

Gamely, we soldiered on toward the big day. There were a

dozen volunteers on duty almost around the clock at "wedding central," the Gouletas offices in Midtown. Western Union assigned us a special staff member just to keep track of the bags of Mailgram invitations going out and more bags of acceptances coming in. We were attracting a glittering guest list of celebrities: other governors; U.S. congressmen and senators who were friends from Hugh Carey's own days in Congress; the mayors of New York and Chicago; and just about every member of the New York state legislature. And those were just the "official" guests. It also seemed to me that we were hosting half the Greek population of the known world. And now we had to contend with a new problem. We had originally booked St. Patrick's Cathedral for the wedding ceremony, but Engie and Hugh could not be married in a Roman Catholic ceremony because of her divorces. So we changed the venue to the Greek Orthodox cathedral Holy Trinity. The Greek rites demanded that the groom have a Greek Orthodox best man. Since the governor had already enlisted his brother Edward for this job, we simply added a second best man, the bride's brother, Nick. It soon became clear to me that for this wedding, we were going to need multiples of *everything.*

The reception was our biggest challenge. The Grand Ballroom of the Waldorf was the only spot in New York that could have held all the guests, but Hugh's son Christopher was banquet manager at the St. Regis Hotel. It's a lovely hotel, but no one public room was large enough for our festivities. We had to plan *two* complete receptions, one in the ballroom on the second floor, another on the roof. It meant we needed two wedding cakes, two state swords to cut them with, two dance bands, two bagpipers, two official toasts to the bride, and two receiving lines. We also needed double the number of security guards. The governor's security people called to moan to me. My biggest contribution to the whole wedding, really, was listening patiently to moans.

April 11 dawned sunny and warm. The huge church was packed. I stood in the rear, where Engie and her party would enter, just in case anything went wrong and they needed me. Michael had decided not to sit in a pew, either, and stood behind me. The moment arrived. The governor stepped out to the altar with his two best men. As Greek tradition demanded, he was wearing a sort of headdress with long ribbons. I suppressed a giggle. Michael whispered in my ear, "There goes the presidency." Engie floated down the aisle with her entourage, wearing virginal white. As soon as the ceremony began, I left to check on preparations at the St. Regis.

I needn't have worried. Everything was perfect, and soon sirens, applause, and shouting in the street outside announced that the wedding party was arriving. We embarked on the double receptions. I spent the next four hours shuttling from the ballroom to the roof garden and back, making sure the two receiving lines were moving, the champagne flowing, and the music playing. We had barely ushered the last guest through the line when it was time to leave for Albany, where the dinner reception was to be held in the Governor's Mansion.

Hugh Carey insisted that we be scrupulous about not spending one penny of state money on this private event, so the two hundred or so guests flying to Albany would be ferried there on private planes. The Gouletas family offered their jet; so did a dozen wealthy Gouletas and Carey friends. We had quite an armada of planes awaiting us at LaGuardia. And I knew this part of the day, at least, could not go wrong because we had carefully assigned the plane seats according to rank: governors, senators, and representatives, with their wives, went to Albany first, followed by mayors, judges, state senators, assemblymen, and so on. It was all carefully planned out, down to the last detail, and we had the passengers lined up at the airfield. We hadn't reckoned with the Greeks. They stormed the barricades and boarded the planes, and the planes took off, leaving the assembled dignitaries standing agape on the tarmac. They were picked up on the second trip to Albany, or maybe the third.

It was almost ten P.M. before all the guests were ferried to the mansion. I remember being so tired that I wanted to put my head down on the table right there, when the governor called my name. He said that he and Engie wanted the first toast of the evening to be to me. He and his bride would remember for all the rest of their married lives what I had done for them.

They were soon separated and then divorced. Like legendary Troy, Governor Hugh Carey was undone by a Greek woman.

CHAPTER 10

The Queen and I

In the summer of 1981, I became the advertising agency for Leona Helmsley. You've heard of her. She was the wife of billionaire real estate giant Harry Helmsley and ran the Helmsley Hotels, including the then new and dazzling Palace in New York. Her previous advertising agency had created a delightful magazine advertising campaign for the hotel, featuring Leona. Photographs showed her peering into the soup pots in the kitchen, supervising the flower arrangements, inspecting the bath towels. The tagline for all the ads was "The only hotel in the world where the Queen stands guard."

When it came to light that she mistreated her help and was sentenced to prison for tax evasion, the press dubbed her "the Queen of Mean." When she died, she cut two of her grandchildren out of her will and left their share to her dog. But don't believe everything you've read about Leona. She was worse than that. I worked for her for seven months, and they were the most terrible months of my life. No man would have put up with it.

Governor Carey introduced me to Leona in early 1981. Leona had invited him to her annual "I'm Just Wild About Harry" birthday bash, one of the most lavish private parties in New York. *Everybody* would be there—Hollywood stars, literary lions, statesmen, the wealthiest people in the world. The governor was concerned that Engie wouldn't know anyone and persuaded Leona to invite Michael and me.

At the party, the guests all wore buttons that proclaimed "I'm Just Wild About Harry." Harry wore the biggest button of all. It said: "I'm Harry." The entire dining room of the Park Lane (a Helmsley hotel, of course) was closed to the public for the evening, beluga caviar was served in containers the size of punch bowls, the orchestra played, the Helmsleys danced, balloons rained down. As we left at the end of the evening, each guest received a "goody bag" with favors, including a music box that played the old song "I'm Just Wild About Harry." Later, I asked Michael how much that party must have cost. "It's like owning a yacht," he said. "If you have to ask, you can't afford it."

Soon afterward, when I was planning the governor's wedding, I wanted to make sure we had a sprinkling of the rich and famous present, and I called Leona to ask if she would share her "Wild About Harry" guest list. She did, discovered I was in advertising, and just a few weeks after the wedding, called and asked me to come and see her in her office at the Palace. At our meeting, she explained that she had just fired her advertising agency and, until she could hire another, needed a little help in marketing the hotels. She was charming; few people I have ever met were more charming than Leona at her best. Promptly at five P.M., Harry Helmsley arrived to escort his wife home. "I have a wonderful idea, Harry," Leona said. "Why don't we set Jane up as our advertising agency? We can give her that nice space in the Graybar Building where Reservations used to be." Harry nodded; clearly, setting up an advertising agency was no big deal for him. Leona patted my cheek. "Do a good job for us, sweetheart, and I'll help you get lots of other clients. I know a lot of really big people. I'll make you into a rich, successful agency." She swept out on Harry's arm, bodyguard in tow. "My door will always be open to you, sweetheart."

I was thrilled at the prospect of running my own advertising agency. What's more, I had been handling the "I Love New York" business at Wells Rich Greene for more than four years and was beginning to wish for something new. Finally, I was sure the Helmsleys indeed *did* know everybody, and I was confident that between Leona and me, my agency could attract a lot of clients.

At home that night, I asked Michael what he thought. "As long as you have me and three square meals a day, what do you have to lose?" Michael advised. I agreed. Few men would make a big decision like changing jobs without checking their Old Boy network. Women still don't have that instinctive reaction, nor do we have as good an Old Girl network. We're getting better, but we're not there yet.

The next day, Harry Helmsley and I signed a letter of agreement, stating that Jane Maas Advertising would be paid ten thousand dollars per month. All that money and free office space, too! I was giddy. Then Michael pointed out gently that I would need to hire some staff. I brought along my secretary, Dolores, who was combination bookkeeper, payroll, human resources, events manager, and guardian angel, hired an art director and a traffic manager to keep track of all the newspaper and magazine insertions. Totaling up the payroll, I realized I was indeed lucky to have Michael and three square meals a day.

Leona showed me the space in the Graybar Building. We walked through what seemed like an acre of empty offices. *Once the agency really gets started, I'll be able to hire dozens of people,* I thought, *maybe* hundreds. Leona pointed to a formidable wooden door that looked like the entrance to a castle, and threw it open. "And this is where Jane Maas Advertising will be." It was one room, about half the size and brightness of my park-view office at Wells Rich Greene. The view from the one dirty, barred window was of the air-conditioning ducts of the adjacent building. *Ah, well,* I rationalized, *it's only temporary.*

Wells Rich Greene threw a big farewell party for me, and the Leona/Jane honeymoon was on. The art director and I dreamed up four different campaigns for the hotels and showed them to Leona. The one she preferred was the campaign that featured her. "I don't like being in the advertising. It's a security risk. I'm too busy to waste my time having photographs taken. But what can I do? If it's good for the hotels, I have to make the sacrifice."

Leona wanted me at her side day and night. She invited me for breakfast in her duplex apartment atop the Park Lane Hotel. I would watch her morning routine: first she swam laps in her private rooftop pool, then Jean Louis, her personal stylist, did her hair and makeup as she munched vitamins and Special K. Finally, her maid helped her into whatever designer outfit she had selected for the day. Leona lectured me about the importance of underwear. "A woman has to look sexy when she gets dressed. And undressed."

She wanted me to join her for lunch every day at the Palace. The first week I worked for her, she stopped at the hotel entrance and beckoned a tiny, terrified Hispanic doorman to come closer. "You. You with the dirt under your fingernails. You're fired. You're out of here right now." Inside she commented to me, "If he'd been wearing the white gloves like he's supposed to, I wouldn't have noticed."

In the dining room, many of the guests recognized Leona and looked impressed. The staff looked terrified. For them, she was like the queen in *Alice in Wonderland* who was always shouting "Off with their heads!" Leona seemed to enjoy firing people, especially the little ones who didn't fight back, and she did it with dispatch. In that first week alone, as I accompanied her on her hotel rounds, she also fired a busboy and a chambermaid. I learned that the staff of her many hotels organized a warning system that would alert them if she was heading their way.

Leona didn't like the way I wore my hair. "Too short, too red." She made me leave my stylist of twenty-five years and go to a trendy, expensive salon. She didn't like the way I dressed, and ordered me to stop wearing pantsuits. She took me to her dressmaker (also expensive) to be fitted for more feminine attire, watched me undress, and hissed, "That's a hideous bra, sweetheart. It looks like a *nursing* bra. Take it off and throw it away." Later, she explained. "You have a very handsome husband. You have to be careful." She didn't like my shoes, and took me to the shoe department at Saks. "How much is this pair?" she asked a salesman. "One hundred fifty dollars," he answered. "I'll give you seventy-five," Leona said. "Never pay retail," she commanded me. "Only little people pay retail."

Meekly, I went along with all this. No man would have stood for it, but I felt it was worth a little personal humiliation to realize the dream of running a big advertising agency of my own. Jane Maas Inc. soon attracted two more clients without Leona's help, but when she found out about it, she didn't like it. Since her dressmaker was right there in the Graybar Building, Leona often paid us surprise visits. If we were working on anything but *her* advertising, there would be a storm. "Why am I paying you all this money to do work for other people?" Clearly, she wasn't going to help me drum up any more new business.

Just as suddenly as it began, the honeymoon began to wane. Leona complained that I didn't have a large enough creative staff to serve her needs. I used my own money to hire freelance copywriters, and brought them to meetings with Leona so she could see what an array of talent we had. Unfailingly, as we walked down the hall to her office, we would hear her shouting at some poor bastard. One after another, the copywriters were frightened into speechlessness. "Your friends don't have much to say for themselves," Leona chided me. "I wouldn't pay them a cent."

One day in early fall Leona called me to say she needed an ad the very next day for the real estate section of the Sunday *New York Times*. She wanted to advertise the penthouse apartments of the Palace, which were available for long-term rental. "On my desk by noon tomorrow," the Queen commanded. I had never written such an ad—I didn't know the lingo and the special abbreviations—but I studied other realty ads, worked hard, and by noon the next day I presented Leona with three different concepts. She threw them on the floor and stamped on them. "My five-year-old grandson can write a better real estate ad than this. Now you just go back and do this over, five hundred times if you have to, but you get back here before this day is over with an ad I can accept."

Leona knew that Michael and I were due to join one of his clients that evening at six for a small, private dinner for Frank Sinatra, before going on to Sinatra's benefit concert at Carnegie Hall. The dinner, coincidentally, was to be at the Palace. I'd told her how excited I was to meet my idol. Now that I was an employee, Leona didn't seem too pleased to have me under her roof as a guest, especially attending a party to which she wasn't invited.

I was back at Leona's office with new ads by four-thirty. She and Harry had their coats on, ready to leave. Was it possible she had forgotten about this crucial ad? Leona glanced at the new copy and handed it to Harry with a shrug. "Amateur hour." She turned to me. "You may have to work all night, but I'm not going to miss that deadline."

Harry was a Quaker, a peacemaker. I don't think he was afraid of his wife, but he always tried to pacify her, tamp down her rages. Now, he glanced at the ad in question, then looked over at me. I think he knew I was close to tears. "It's not that bad," he told Leona mildly. "Let's run it and see what happens." I was pathetically grateful. (Two weeks later, an Arab potentate rented both the apartments. I never knew if he saw my ad.)

Just a few weeks later, Leona rejected the photographs taken for one of the hotels and refused to pay the photographer I had hired. "Tell him to sue me," she snapped. "Tell him to get in line." The photographer sued, and Leona countersued both the photographer and me. She telephoned me in a fury. "How dare you sue me?" "Gosh, Leona," I said sweetly. "I'm not suing you. You're suing *me.*"

The judge at the trial found the photographs not only acceptable, but downright excellent. Leona's attorney, listening to the verdict, looked like a victim heading for the scaffold. I was sorry for him; I knew exactly how he felt.

The daily browbeatings got worse, and I began to walk the few blocks from my office to Leona's saying Hail Marys and praying that the meeting wouldn't be too degrading. My feisty Irish secretary, Dolores, kept telling me, "Tell her to take her ads and shove them up her royal rear. You're worth ten of her." I desperately wanted to quit, but there were three people working for me (including Dolores)—three people I had taken from secure jobs and who were now depending on me. I began to put out feelers for other jobs, and felt a few nibbles: both Ogilvy & Mather and Wells Rich Greene said there might be a spot for me to come back to, and another agency, Muller Jordan Weiss, wanted to discuss possibilities. Still, any of those moves would mean dismissing my little staff.

Michael insisted that we take our usual October week of vacation that year in Venice. The weather was glorious, we had a room overlooking the Grand Canal, Michael was ebullient, and I was miserable. I called the office every day to see if they had heard from Leona. They hadn't, and that seemed so ominous that I told Michael I wanted to go home a few days early. Michael stood firm. "Leona has already ruined your holiday, but I'm not going to let her ruin mine." I stayed in Venice and thought about the way she bullied busboys and doormen, about her disdain for "little people," and, blessedly, I got mad. I am only five feet tall, but all my life I have said to people, "I'm little, but I'm tough." I made a date to see Leona in her office the day after we returned.

"It's not working, Leona. We both know that. I'll be glad to give you sixty days' notice while you find another agency, but the sooner we end this, the better." Like many bullies, Leona backed down when confronted. She was suddenly her old charming self again. "It's better to make a clean break, sweetheart, and this way we can still be friends. So today can be your last day." She stood at her desk, indicating that the meeting was over. "My door will always be open to you, sweetheart." As I left, I could hear her door shut behind me.

Leona was a woman of many paradoxes. She was born Leona Mindy Rosenthal to Polish Jewish immigrants on July 4, 1920. (Harry always lighted up the Empire State Building—one of his many New York properties—in red, white, and blue to celebrate her birthday.) I think she was obsessed with money all her life. She dropped out of Hunter College as a sophomore to take a modeling job. As a twice-divorced, struggling single mom at the age of forty, she went to work as a receptionist at a real estate firm, and rose to senior vice president in seven years. Before she met and married Harry Helmsley, Leona was independently wealthy on commissions. The Helmsleys had billions, yet Leona always haggled with merchants, refused to pay retail, and cheated on her taxes.

Leona had hundreds of superbly styled daytime outfits from designers like Dior, Yves Saint Laurent, and Bill Blass.

Yet in the evenings she often wore fussy, pouffy taffeta gowns codesigned by Leona and the little seamstress she housed in the Graybar Building.

She traveled in high society but was unsure of herself socially and depended on other people to know the correct thing to do. Usually it was the last person she had spoken to. I was at lunch one day at the Palace with Leona and her proper British general manager. She ordered for all of us—the newest item on the menu: *Swedish* smoked salmon, she told us. It arrived in razor-thin slices, and the manager, who knew his salmon, mentioned that this particular variety was meant to be served thick. Leona scowled, then called the maître d' over and scolded him. "It's embarrassing to me when this establishment doesn't know how to do things right. Take it away."

The very next day we were back at the Palace for lunch, this time with Leona's brother, Alvin Rosenthal, who worked for her as manager of the residential Carlton House. Leona again ordered the Swedish salmon. It came in thick slices just as prescribed. Mr. Rosenthal laughed. "God, what is the kitchen coming to? This is supposed to be served paper-thin." Leona, looking thunderous, beckoned the maître d'. He could tell from her expression that something was terribly wrong. It couldn't possibly be the salmon, could it? "Take this salmon away," Leona commanded, "and learn how to slice it the way it should be served. Paper thin." The maître d' bowed deeply, apologized, and removed the offending fish.

Her business relationships were mercurial; so were her friendships. She liked her director of marketing so much that when his wife became mysteriously ill, Leona flew them in her private jet to see a specialist. Within the year, he was out of favor. She wept as she told me of her son's heart ailment, but when he died some months later, she immediately changed her will, disinheriting her daughter-in-law.

I suspect Leona had a carefully constructed outer shell that protected a deep vulnerability underneath. She never wanted anyone to get too close, or they might pierce her armor. Leona Helmsley, one of the wealthiest women in the world, the Queen of the Palace, never got over being a poor little Jewish kid from Brooklyn.

I went back to the office and announced that Jane Maas Inc. was no more, effective that day, but everyone would receive three months' severance pay. I knew it would come out of the Maas family pockets, but my little staff deserved fair treatment. Later that week, as I was packing up and closing the office, I came across the music box Leona had given as a favor on the night of Harry's birthday. It no longer played "I'm Just Wild About Harry." It had wound down.

CHAPTER 11

Have You Really Come Such a Long Way, Baby?

Almost immediately, the Muller Jordan Weiss advertising agency recruited me to be president. The first day of my new job, I arrived early at 666 Fifth Avenue, elated to be heading an established, respected New York agency with big-name clients like Monsanto and McGraw-Hill. In my sunny office, the movers were still arranging furniture. "Where do you want the desk, lady?" one asked me. "Under the windows, please," I directed. But it wasn't quite right there, so I asked them to shift it to the far wall. I decided I liked the first solution better, and with apologies, asked them to put it under the windows again. The mover was exasperated. "Jeez, lady, why don't you wait for your boss to come in and let *him* decide where he wants his desk."

I remembered the tagline for Virginia Slims, the cigarette brand created especially for women—"You've come a long way, baby." Maybe we really hadn't. They say the line was written by a man. That was at the height of the women's liberation movement, when men, who were still making all the decisions, thought that women wanted our own cigarettes, our own hotel rooms (decorated in pink), and our own banks. So men created them, and of course they all failed. Nobody asked us.

My seven months of servitude with Leona happened thirty years ago. Today, when I talk about my time with her, women look at me with sympathy and understanding, men with disbelief. How could I have allowed myself to be so humiliated, so tormented, and so badly paid for such a long time? And I was no beginner at that point. I had been creative director at two world-class agencies, turned out winning advertising for some of the biggest companies in the world, and run one of the most successful tourism campaigns in history. Leona made me feel small and frightened and ultimately, glory be, she made me angry.

The stay-at-home moms of the 1950s and 1960s were angry because they were trapped. They trapped themselves, which made it worse, because they graduated from Bryn Mawr and Radcliffe and Vassar and Smith, got married, and . . . vanished. They had no identity apart from being somebody's wife and somebody's mother. So, as they hung their laundry on the line in their suburban backyards, they gnashed their teeth.

The "you can have it all" moms of the 1970s and 1980s were furious because we had brought this all down on our own heads. A commercial of the day showed one of the new breed of women managing the world. The song went: "I can bring home the bacon / Fry it up in a pan / And never let you forget you're a man." A lot of us believed that we were indeed capable of being perfect wives, wonderful mothers, and outstanding career women. We were supposed to perform a sort of triage as to which role took precedence at any given moment. What got fried up in the process was the woman. We didn't think we had done any of the three roles as well as we should have. So, as we sat in our apartment house laundry rooms late at night, we sobbed and snarled.

The "let's be realistic" moms of the 1990s and 2000s are outraged because it's still not working—and what's worse, they don't know how to fix it. So, as they multitask, checking their iPads for messages from the office, making out low-cal, low-carb shopping lists, and watching their children play violent games on Xbox, they curse the system.

Maybe the women who entered the advertising world of the sixties really were mad. We were probably crazy to think we could break into such a male-dominated world, where the only sure way for a woman to become a copywriter was to start as a secretary and write ads on a speculative basis nights and weekends, for free.

I do know for sure that we were angry. Almost every woman I interviewed about working during the *Mad Men* era—especially working mothers—told me how angry she felt about being torn apart, and how much she reproached herself for underperforming in all her roles.

The interviews that surprised me the most, however, were those with full-time working mothers *today*. Almost every one of them is guilty, frustrated, overwhelmed, and, yes, angry. They agree that, overall, husbands are more helpful and working conditions more flexible than they were fifty years ago, but when the chips are down, they ask, who stays home with a sick child?

Shelly Lazarus underscores the difficulty. “It’s hard,” she told me just a few months ago, and sighed and repeated, “It’s hard.” She talked about a breakfast she hosted recently for a group of women on the topic they had requested: “How to Balance Careers and Motherhood.” “What was obvious was that each of these young women felt that every other woman in the world was functioning as a senior vice president of marketing and wife and mother and throwing dinner parties and doing things in the community and they were having absolutely no problem but that I—the woman speaking—I’m dying. I’m drowning. I can’t do this. I’m inadequate. What I realized at the end of the breakfast was that all of these women were experiencing the same thing. It’s just that they never had the opportunity, they never felt empowered before, to talk about it with other women.”

Laurel Cutler agrees. “There is still a war between women who don’t stay home and women who do stay home, and I think that’s tragic. The guilt is intense on both sides of the conflict.” Cutler, not knowing it, reprises Lazarus. “It’s hard. It’s very hard.”

Here’s another problem. Women are lousy mentors; we say we are giving the newbies a helping hand, but our hearts are not in it. (I know I’m going to get a lot of irate mail about this, but it’s true.) The most successful women in our business, the ones who rival men, don’t have time to mentor. And besides, there’s a little undercurrent of feeling that says, “I’ve made it on my own; why should *you* expect to be carried?” Because I am a former New York Advertising Woman of the Year, I get to vote on the new winner every fall. “Community service” is one of the criteria for nomination, and mentoring other women fills this bill. So we show up for events that welcome new women into the New York advertising world, and we hire interns, and we speak at our alma maters. Secretly, however, most successful women are a bit jealous and even fearful of the eager young things who want to elbow us out.

What about children? How hard was it for my children, or any kids of the sixties, to have a working mother? Mary Lou Quinlan, founder and CEO of a leading women's marketing company, remembers what it was like in Philadelphia when she was a child. "My beautiful, redheaded mother was executive secretary to the CEO of a big advertising agency. I thought my mother was so wonderful, going off to work every morning at seven-thirty, just like my father. She loved her job, and that's all we talked about at our dinner table—her day at the agency, the glamour, the excitement. Before I was nine I knew about new business pitches, media plans, and storyboards."

Quinlan remembers that very few of her fourth-grade classmates had full-time working mothers. "Most kids went home for lunch, but my brother and I had to bring our lunch and eat it at school. I thought that was a special privilege. Then one day, the nun teaching our class said, 'I want all the children whose mothers have to work to raise your hands.' So, out of a class of sixty, three hands went up. The nun said, 'Look around at these children and feel sorry for them because their mothers can't be home to take care of them.' " Quinlan quickly assured me she was not "nun-bashing." "Any teacher in any school during that era could easily have said the same thing. But the nun's comment stunned me. I was proud that my mother worked."

My daughters each have very different attitudes toward my

career. I'm not sure whether it's due to the four-year age difference or the fact that working mothers were sort of lunatic fringe when Kate was in grade school, more socially acceptable by the time Jenny got there. Whatever the reason, Kate quietly resents all the hours I put in, and makes sure she is not giving her own daughter short shrift. "I just don't remember you being there, Mom," she tells me. Jen, on the other hand, reminds me that for most of her friends, I was the heroine they wanted *their* mothers to be.

How about children of working mothers *today*? Most mothers work, and nobody goes home for lunch anymore. Yet some children take their mother's absence in stride while others struggle with it every day. Psychologist Alisa Greenwald says that children who cope best are those "with a secure attachment to their moms, kids who feel safe." Dr. Greenwald adds that children who have problems tend to be those who "get bounced around from place to place—the suitcase after-school kids. Children with a stable, loving presence who *regularly* fills in for the mother handle it better."

Yet mothers worry endlessly about children resenting their absence. Tina Fey, in her loony, luminous autobiography *Bossypants,* writes, "The topic of working moms is a tap-dance recital in a minefield." The star of NBC's *Saturday Night Live* and *30 Rock* recounts how her heart sank when her preschool-age daughter checked out of the library a book called *My Working Mom*. It has a cartoon witch on the cover and there's a lot about the witch mother being very busy and having to fly away to a lot of meetings. The witch's child says it's hard having a working mom, but in the end, she can't picture her mother any other way. Later, Fey asked her daughter if reading the book made her feel any better about the fact that her mother worked. The child replied: "Mommy, I can't read. I thought it was a Halloween book."

Ad woman Karen Francis is another member of the slightly younger cohort, a Dartmouth graduate of 1984 who quickly rose into the top ranks of the male automotive fraternity at General Motors. Francis has said she admires women "who are coming to grips with the fact that they can't be everything. I have women coming into my office and admitting—and it's very hard to admit—that they can't be a superperformer at work and a supermom and a superwife and a super everything." She added that for many of them the right choice is to slow down a little and devote more time to their children.

It's almost too easy to say that things are better for working women today. I keep hearing that it is actually *harder.* "The world is more punishing today," Mary Lou Quinlan believes. "Brand managers and CMOs are under more pressure. Ad agencies are scared stiff of the account turnover and are asking fewer people to put in longer hours. Companies can't make allowances for life the way they used to."

Curiously enough, the Internet and instant communication are making it harder, too. Smartphones keep us in touch with the office 24/7. I keep receiving e-mails from colleagues announcing that they will be out of the office on such-and-such dates and will have "limited access to e-mail." As long as there is still an iPhone within reach, where on earth do you go to achieve limited access to e-mail?

Many women have told me we bring "working-mother stress" on ourselves. Judy Lotas, an agency founder and mother, has said, "We try to do it all ourselves and we shouldn't. A lot of guys in the marriage relationship feel left out, because they want to help and women won't let them. If there were more genuine sharing, I think it would be so healthy. Everybody would have a better time, including the kids."

The respected educator Edes Gilbert, who headed Manhattan's top-notch Spence School, believes women are wired differently. "Men solve the child-rearing problem by saying, 'Hire somebody.' Women find this goes against their deepest instincts. To feel that you are abandoning this most primal of all relationships creates profound guilt. So we refuse to give responsibility to a surrogate. It's the mothers today who are having the problems. The fathers are still going on their merry way. Tra-la!"

My friend Patricia Carbine, cofounder with Gloria Steinem of *Ms.* magazine, feels that women today are still being penalized. She had a lot to say in an interview filmed by the History Channel and Advertising Women of New York. "When I am with young women, one question arises fairly quickly: 'How am I going to handle being a successful worker and a mother and a wife?' It is very rare for a man to stand up and ask that question. Until we see men moving into the areas where women have always resided—as women have moved into male areas—women are going to be stuck with two jobs. And exhaustion." Carbine added that she is disappointed that the advertising industry has not stepped up well enough as yet to the task of presenting men in commercials and print ads as part of the family, a contributing member of the household.

Edes Gilbert connects the increasing guilt of working mothers to the rise of today's helicopter mom, constantly hovering over her children. "In the good old days," she says, "if a child came home with an F on a paper, the mother would give the child a good scolding. Now, the mother calls the school and gives the *teacher* a good scolding. And if she's really upset, she calls the principal, too." Gilbert adds that the higher a woman stands professionally, the more likely she is to hover. It makes sense: the executive mom likes to be in charge.

Many colleges today have established elaborate rituals to drive away the helicopter moms after the obligatory welcoming ceremonies. One school has a welcome to students/good-bye to parents ceremony. The freshmen sit on one side of the auditorium, the parents sit on the other, and the administrators, in their robes, sit in the middle. When the speeches are over, the administrators stand and turn their backs on the parents, forming a forbidding black line, and escort the students out. One of those freshmen mothers told me she was deeply offended. "How dare they turn their backs on us, the people paying the bills?"

I still give a lot of my time to Bucknell and spend a fair amount of time on the Bucknell campus. Many students, male and female, speak with their mothers five and six times a day or more. "Hi, I'm heading to poli-sci. Call you when it's over." "Hi, just came from poli-sci." They tell me it's simply an ingrained habit. Cell phones suddenly made it possible for working mothers to assuage their guilt somewhat with lots of "How are you doing?" calls. The children are continuing the practice into young adulthood, and maybe beyond.

There's also a new trend I have been spotting. Many working mothers I know, women who have become successful executives and earn top salaries, are quitting and staying home when their children reach high school. They tell me they don't need the money, their husbands are now at the top of *their* professions, and they want to devote themselves full-time to the children. These revelations shock me. What does this decision say about the importance of their careers?

Have we come such a long way? I compared the notes from my interviews with women who were working mothers in the sixties and those who are working mothers today. Eerily, they use almost exactly the same words. "I'm pulled in so many directions. I'm not doing *anything* as well as I should." It's a time warp. Maybe we haven't come such a long way after all.

For sure, we still have a long way to go.

Epilogue: The War Over *Mad Men*

Mad Men has split the advertising world into two camps: those who love it and those who don't. Charlie Moss, whose creative good taste is flawless, represents one school of thought. He told me, "It's my favorite show. It's so well crafted. Maybe it's not fully accurate, but it comes closer than any other I've seen." Ken Roman represents the other camp. He says, "It's just a soap opera set in an advertising agency. The way *The Sopranos* was a soap opera with a Mafia backdrop."

That creative tornado George Lois is one of the series' most outspoken critics. He feels that *Mad Men* misrepresents the advertising industry by ignoring the impact of the creative revolution. In doing that, he believes, the show is "a lie." The big Greek, still creating compelling advertising in his late seventies, invited me to his estate-size Greenwich Village apartment for an interview. In deference to my age and gender, he said "fuck" only eight or ten times in two hours. I was enchanted.

"They don't get it," he said, referring to the creators of

Mad Men. "They are missing the *passion* we had. How hard we worked. How much we liked each other. And most important, what *fun* we had."

Mary Wells Lawrence talks about how *young* we were back then. "In the sixties the world went young. Young people revolutionized the movies, music, advertising—most of the Western world's cultures. Agencies were great fun because we were making changes right and left. Young people had great power and respect in the sixties, and being in the agency business was very glamorous."

Those opinions are shared by every sixties survivor I have spoken with. The television show doesn't capture the most important creative secret of all. We were having a *wonderful* time. We were in love with advertising.

Mad women. Mad men. Mad days. I had a wonderful time, too. Looking back, there isn't a single thing I would do differently.

Except I wouldn't work for Leona.

And I'd still like to see Pine Valley.

Acknowledgments

Three people were part of this book from the very first day.

Ken Roman gave me the idea. My old friend and co-author of *How to Advertise,* he wrote the fascinating and definitive biography of David Ogilvy, published in 2008. One day in late 2010, he remarked to me that there were lots of other books that could be written about the *real* mad men of Madison Avenue, and that several writers were already embarked on them. It occurred to me that nobody was writing a book about the real mad *women,* and I asked Ken if he would again like to collaborate. Ken declined, with his usual grace, declaring that this was my book to write, but he has been there for me with generous advice at every turn.

Tom Dunne was a young editor at St. Martin's Press in 1975 when he agreed to publish *How to Advertise.* The manuscript had been turned down by sixteen other publishers; then Tom said yes. It's still in print almost forty years, three editions, and 160,000 copies later. Well, Tom also said an immediate yes to *Mad Women,* and has beamed his infectious Irish enthusiasm and editorial smarts on the project without stint.

My longtime agent, Lynn Nesbit, is the third early supporter, and from the beginning gave me the care, insights, and honest advice she is famous for. I came to expect her regular "idea of the week" telephone calls.

Three other people played major roles. Margaret Smith and Anne Bensson, editors at Thomas Dunne Books, were my cheerleaders. Every author has those awful moments of knowing you have just written the most boring chapter in the history of the world. Unfailingly at those times, Anne and Margaret would pop up to tell me that they loved it. They were wonderful at knowing when I should fill out a description, add to a character, or explain a motive. They are the shapers of *Mad Women.*

My "mermaid sister" in London, Susan Griggs, read the manuscript with an artist's eye and a writer's soul. She had a comment on every page, and improved every page she touched. Susan also saved me from making sometimes hilarious and occasionally painful blunders.

Many mad women—and a few mad men—were generous in giving me interviews and candid in their recollections. I especially want to thank several people who, in addition, wrote reviews: Mary Wells Lawrence for her delightful foreword; and Patricia Bosworth, Laurel Cutler, Jerry Della Femina, Linda Bird Francke, Shelly Lazarus, Bob Liodice, George Lois, Bruce McCall, and Anne Tolstoi Wallach Maslon.

I am grateful for interviews to: Lee Aiges, Olivia Altschuler, Rena Bartos, John Blaney, Don Dixon, Peter Hochstein, Ann Iverson, Jack Kennard, Elaine Kerner, Joan Lipton, Sally Minard, Charlie Moss, Roger Proulx, Mary Lou Quinlan, Marikay and Joel Raphaelson, Elaine Reiss, Ellen and Ken Roman, Marcella Rosen, Gloria Wells Sidnam, Daisy Sinclair, Lee Thuna, Anne Tolstoi Wallach Maslon, Ellie Watrous, Bill Weed, and Tony Weir.

Advertising Women of New York and History, the cable channel, gave me access to additional interview material with a number of women, including Pat Carbine, Karen Francis, and Judy Lotas.

Several people shared their memories and/or their expertise. Carmen Dyce ("Mabel"), who helped me relive important moments of our shared lives; Edes Gilbert, friend and former head of New York's Spence School; and psychologist Dr. Alisa Greenwald. Early readers who urged me on included Barbara Sweeney, Georgianne Ensign Kent, and my sister, Susan Weston.

The extraordinary Laura Bonington Masse was my personal Chief Marketing Officer for this book. Laura developed a marketing plan, attended meetings, and crackled with ideas for promotions and partnerships. Suzan Couch, Steve Lance, and Chris Moseley contributed a wealth of marketing suggestions. Jennifer Maas, Gigi Marino, Chris Hill Killough, and especially Lauren Hesse and Paul Hochman of St. Martin's Press tutored me in social media. Andrew Beierle taught me about Web sites, and Harriet Causbie, Ogilvy's head librarian, and Chris Fry of Bucknell University went out of their way to unearth photos.

I am grateful to Heather Florence for being the kind of lawyer who offered solutions instead of obstacles, and to Sibylle Kazeroid for being the kind of copy editor who never took my punctuation, my spelling, or my memory for granted.

acknowledgments

Michael Leu took the charming photo of me, and Stanley Lakhchakov got up hours earlier than usual to style my hair.

So many people at St. Martin's Press and Macmillan have done so much. I am indebted to Sally Richardson, Matthew Baldacci, Kim Bouchard, Laura Clark, Mariann Donato, Stephanie Hargadon, Meg Drislane, Audrey Campbell, Dana Trocker, and scores of other people who made *Mad Women* happen.

Finally, my thanks to my dear ones for understanding that during these months of writing I was often unavailable or distracted: Kate and Jenna Maas, Jennifer and Allen Jones, Carmen Dyce, and Harry R. Garvin—I love you.

Index

Abraham, F. Murray, 41
Adventures of an Advertising Woman (Maas), 151–52
Advertising Hall of Fame, 37, 55, 103
advertising industry. *See also* creative revolution, advertising; sexism; women, career
agency churn in, 146–48
alcohol consumption in, 93–111
BIG IDEA concept in, 48, 138–40
commercial shoots for, 39–42, 101, 162–64
continuing character devices in, 145–46
creative revolution in, 135–50, 213–14
day in the life of, 1–25
decor, office, in, 120–21
diversity in, 131–32
dress/attire in, 113–18
homosexuality and, 132–33
mnemonic devices in, 7–8, 144–45
presentation "bake-offs" in, 148–50
salaries associated with, 33, 51–69
schools of, 5–6, 7–8, 135–41, 144–47
sex as selling tool of, 157, 164–71
sexism in, 4, 6, 8–9, 16–17, 24–25, 29–30, 46–49, 51–69, 71–92, 113–19, 121–23, 129–31, 133–34, 157–60, 203–12
sexual activity in, 27–49
smoking habits in, 103–11
technology's impact on, 119–20, 125–26
truth in, 161–64
Advertising to Women (agency), 167–68

index

Advertising Women of New York, 206, 210
Aiges, Lee, 71
Aim, 159
Ajax, 145
Alberghetti, Anna Maria, 160
alcohol consumption
  alcoholism and, 102–3
  on *Mad Men,* 93–94, 98, 102
  at Ogilvy & Mather, 94–95, 98–103
  women and, 102–3
Alka-Seltzer, 66, 135
American Express, 6, 42, 62–63, 160
American Federation of Television and Radio Artists, 62
American Institute of Architects, 89–90
American Motors, 138
Ammens, 12
The Amy Vanderbilt Complete Book of Etiquette (Baldrige), 184
Anacin, 7, 135–36, 146–47, 177
attire, office, 113–14
  hats in, 115–16, 118
  miniskirts in, 117–18
  pantsuits in, 116–17
Aviance, 167–68
Avis, 7, 138

Baldrige, Letitia, 184–86
Ban, 169
Bartos, Rena, 55
Benson & Hedges, 66, 138
Benton & Bowles, 146
Bernbach, Bill, 5, 118, 137–38
Bic, 66
The Big Idea (Lois), 168
A Big Life in Advertising (Wells), 64
Blaney, John, 60
Bossypants (Fey), 208
Bounty, 145
Bouquet de France (Chamberlain), 124
Braniff, 64, 165
Brown, Helen Gurley, 164–65
Broxident, 148
Brynner, Yul, 179
Bucknell University, 40, 57, 109, 132–33, 211
  sexism at, 73–78
Burton, Richard, 169
Business Council for the ERA, 90

Calvin Klein, 165
Campbell's, 146, 163
Carbine, Patricia, 210
Carey, Christopher, 187
Carey, Hugh, 173–74, *178,* 181–89, 192
Carter, Jimmy, 90–91
Catlett, Mary Jo, 14–15
Chamberlain, Samuel, 124
Charlie and the Chocolate Factory (Dahl), 153
Charmin, 146
child rearing, 2–4, 11, 15–16, 23–24, 90–92, 123, 204. *See also* housewives; women, career
  child care and, 80–89, 205

contemporary, 205–12
educational bias towards, 72–78
working mother stigma and, 71–72, 81–82
workplace bias regarding, 78–83, 113, 205, 210
Claiborne, Craig, 127
Clairol, 8–9, 17, 20, 51–52, 117
Clark, Howard, 63
Cleopatra, 169
Collins, Michael, 129
Comet, 145, 161
commercial shoots
alcohol consumption on, 101
crews associated with, 162–63
sexual trysts on, 39–42
truth in advertising and, 163–64
Confessions of an Advertising Man (Ogilvy), 17, 21, 130, 140, 151
continuing character devices, 145–46
Cooper, Gary, 153
Cornell, 57, 109
Cosmopolitan, 164–65
Courrèges, André, 117
creative revolution, advertising, 213–14
agency churn in, 146–48
BIG IDEA concept and, 48, 138–40
continuing character devices in, 145–46
honesty as element of, 137–38
irreverence as element of, 136–37
market research and, 140–44
presentation "bake-offs" in, 148–50
story appeal and, 140
Cronyn, Hume, 179
Crosland, Felicity, 155
Cutler, Laurel, 55, 71, 206

Dahl, Roald, 152–55
Daily News, 174
Dancer Fitzgerald Sample, 30–31
Della Femina, Jerry, 39, 56, 94, 104, 109, 135, 147, 151–52
Della Femina Travisano & Partners, 39
Department of Commerce, New York, 174–77
Devereux, Fran, 101
Dinkins, David, 186
Dove, 3, 8, 9–11, 14–16, 23, 42, 54, 61, 145, 147, 157–59
gender stereotypes and, 157–59
Doyle Dane Bernbach, 5, 7, 118, 136–38, 147–48
Drackett Company, 17, 23
Dragoti, Stan, 173, 176
Drano, 6, 17, 22, 23, 145
Dyce, Carmen "Mabel," 20, 23, 124
background of, 86
child care by, 3, 11, 80–81, 83–89, 123
Dyce, Locksley, 86, 88–89
Dyson, John, 175, 180

Elements of Style (Strunk/White), 95
Elliott, Elly, 17

index

Elliott, John, Jr. "Jock," 16–17, 44, 170
Equal Rights Amendment, 90–91
Ernst, Lois Geraci, 167–68
Esquire, 168–69
Evans, Nick, 17
Everyman (Roth), 40
Ex-Lax, 145

Fawcett-Majors, Farrah, 167
Federal Communications Commission, 161, 167
The Feminine Mystique (Friedan), 73, 85
feminist movement, 55, 131
  stereotypes in advertising and, 157–60, 210
Ferguson, Jim, 99–100
Fey, Tina, 208–9
Foote, Cone & Belding, 8, 51–52
Ford, George, 183
Ford, Gerald, 174
Four Seasons, New York, 43–44, 127–28
Foxworth, Jo, 103
Francis, Karen, 209
Francke, Linda Bird, 27–28, 53, 82, 95
Friedan, Betty, 53, 73, 85, 167
From Those Wonderful Folks Who Gave You Pearl Harbor (Della Femina), 39, 135, 151
Funicello, Annette, 161
General Foods, 8, 43, 99–100
  market research by, 141–44, 158, 161
  Neal campaign by, 152–55, 158
  parties by, 38
Gernreich, Rudi, 117
Gilbert, Edes, 210–11
Gillette, 60
Giraudoux, Jean, 74
Giuliani, Rudy, 186
Glaser, Milton, 173, 177
Good Seasons, 5, 159, 161
Gouletas, Evangeline "Engie," 182–89, 192
Grayson, Eugene Debs "Gene," 11, 15, 61–62, 130, 132, 147
  advertising approach of, 7–8
  day in the life of, 4–9, 12–13, 20, 22–24
Green Giant, 146
Greenwald, Alisa, 208
Grey agency, 149
Greyhound Bus, 149
Guarnotta, Gloria, 131

Haines Lundberg & Waehler, Architects, 128
Heekin, Jim, 8–9, 16, 17–20, 132
Heidi Chronicles, 43
Helmsley, Harry, 191–93, 197, 201
Helmsley, Leona, 191–201, 214
Herzbrun, David, 148
Higbee, Bob, 95–96
Hochstein, Peter, 107, 120
Hoff, Ron, 110
Holy Trinity Church, New York, 187–88

housewives, 204
housework by, 122–24
perception of, 55, 122
How to Advertise (Maas/Roman), 64–66, 166, 171

"I Love New York" campaign, 89, 93–94, 182–83, 193
components of, 173–74, 176–77
market research behind, 175, 179
results of, 179–81
Imperial margarine, 145

James and the Giant Peach (Dahl), 153
Jane Maas Advertising, 191–201
Jasper, Jay, 171
Jell-O, 28
Johnson, Arte, 41–42
Johnson, "Mr. Sam," 151
Johnson Wax, 149–51
J. Walter Thompson agency, 32–33, 55, 59, 115, 122
diversity, employee, at, 132

Karmen, Steve, 174, 177
Kelly Award, 171
Kennedy, Jackie, 118, 184
Kennedy, John F., 118
Kershaw, Andrew, 43–44, 122, 132
Kershaw, Mary, 43–44
The King of Madison Avenue (Roman), 35
Koch, Ed, 175, *178*
Korda, Reva, 16–17, 83–84, 116–17, 132
Kotex, 6
Kriendler, "Colonel Bob," 128
Kriendler, Florence, 128

Langella, Frank, 179
Laugh-In, 42
Lawrence, Harding, 64, 69
Lawrence, Mary Wells, 64–69, 90, 110, 135, 147, 174, 181, 184, 214. *See also* Wells Rich Greene
Lazarus, Shelly, 52–53, 56, 66, 73, 79, 206
Lever Brothers, 10, 20, 42, 48, 61, 99, 157–59
market research by, 141
parties by, 37–38
Lexington, Hotel, New York, 28
Lipton, Joan, 27, 63
Lois, George, 120, 147–48, 159, 168–69, 213
Look magazine, 96
Loren, Sophia, 161
Lotas, Judy, 209
Lucky Strike, 105, 136

Maas, Carl, 129
Maas, Jane, *19, 65, 74, 166*
agency launch by, 191–201
cancer of, 88
Carey wedding and, 181–89
day in the life of, 1–25
education of, 57, 73–78

Maas, Jane (*continued*)
Helmsley's association with, 191–201, 214
marriage of, 96–98
at Muller Jordan Weiss, 152, 165, 198, 203
at Ogilvy & Mather, 1–25, 33–49, 61–63, 82–84, 89, 92, 94–95, 98–103, 106–7, 110, 116–17, 119–21, 128, 130–32, 138–44, 149–55, 157–65, 169, 171, 198
sexual harassment of, 46–49
smoking habit of, 104–8, 125
at Wells Rich Greene, 64–69, 89–91, 93–94, 104, 119, 122, 173–83, 193–94, 198
work background of, 10–11, 57–58
Maas, Jenny, 23, 36, 111, 127
birth of, 21, 80, 105
marriage of, 88
working mothers and, 3, 24, 80–81, 83–89, 139–40, 208
Maas, Kate, 15, 36, 119, 127
birth of, 21, 80, 104, 105
working mothers and, 2–3, 24, 72, 80–81, 83–89, 208
Maas, Michael, 17, *18,* 21, 23–25, 36–38, 75, 115–16, 119, 192, 197, 198–99
career support by, 1–2, 20, 85, 89–90, 93
Carey wedding and, 182–84, 188
child care and, 83–84
death of, 69, 88
dining/entertaining by, 122–25, 127–28, 133–34
marriage of, 96–98
smoking and, 105–8, 125
Maas, Peter, 29, 96, 128
Mabel. *See* Dyce, Carmen "Mabel"
Mad Men (television show), ix, 42, 124, 126–27, 152
advertising approaches used on, 136
alcohol consumption on, 93–94, 98, 102
costumes on, 114–15, 118
critics of, 213–14
diversity of characters on, 131–32
props/decor of, 119, 120–21
sex portrayal on, 27, 29–30
smoking on, 103–5, 109
working women and, 52, 54, 72, 75, 91
Young & Rubicam's association to, 27
The Madwoman of Chaillot, 74
Magazine Publishers Association, 171
Margittai, Tom, 44
marijuana use, 109–11
market research, 55, 140–44
Martin & Lipton Agency, 63
Martin, Pat, 63
Matrix Award, 185
Maxim coffee, 6, 7–8, 21, 145, 163
gender stereotypes and, 158–59
Neal campaign for, 128, 152–55, 158
Maxwell House, 43, 122, 145, 159
Maytag, 145
McCann-Erickson, 71

Mercedes-Benz, 6, 160
Meyer, Sandra, 43–44
The Mickey Mouse Club, 161
Midas mufflers, 66
Milky Way, 6
mnemonic devices, 7–8, 144–45
Moss, Charlie, 66, 173, 176, 213
Ms. magazine, 210
Muller Jordan Weiss, 152, 165, 198, 203
My Working Mom, 208

Namath, Joe, 159, 167
Name That Tune, 10–11, 57–59, 97, 109
National Airline, 167
National Organization for Women (NOW), 158–59, 167
Neal, Patricia, 128–29
  Maxim commercials by, 152–55, 158, 161
New York, State of, 66, 89, 93–94, 173–83, 193
The New York Times, 13, 86, 124, 127, 136, 196
Nightingale-Bamford school, New York City, 3–4, 15, 72, 81
NOW. *See* National Organization for Women
Noxzema, 167

Ogilvy, David, 21–22, 53, 62, 82, 99, 101, 120, 155, 181
  advertising style of, 7, 55, 136–37, 138, 140–41, 148–49, 171
  employee recruiting by, 7, 46, 95, 132, 147–48
  gender bias and, 17, 54, 79–80, 103, 117
  Magic Lantern presentations by, 12–14
  office sex and, 34, 37, 49
  paradoxes of, 35–36, 130
Ogilvy, Herta, 35–37
Ogilvy & Mather
  advertising approach by, 7, 55, 136–37, 138, 140–44, 147–51, 171
  alcohol consumption at, 94–95, 98–103
  attire at, 115–17
  a day in the life at, 1–25
  decor at, 121
  diversity at, 131–32
  Maas's work with, 1–25, 33–49, 61–63, 82–84, 89, 92, 94–95, 98–103, 106–7, 110, 116–17, 119–21, 128, 130–32, 138–44, 149–55, 157–65, 169, 171, 198
  marijuana use at, 110
  market research by, 55, 140–44
  nepotism and, 17, 54
  Rose's Room at, 98–101
  sex in advertising by, 169–71
  sexual liaisons at, 30, 33–34, 37–44
  stereotypes promoted by, 157–61
  technology and, 119–20
  women's promotion/salaries at, 17, 52–57, 60–63, 71
  working mothers at, 79–84, 89, 91–92

index

Ogilvy on Advertising (Ogilvy), 171
Olivetti, 159
Open Pit, 160
Owens Corning, 160

Paco Rabanne, 170–71
Palmolive, 145
Papert Koenig Lois, 120
Pepperidge Farm, 54
Phillips, Bill, 45–46, 100
Pillsbury, 146
Pine Valley Golf Club, New Jersey, 24–25, 214
Polykoff, Shirley, 51–52
Potter, Beatrix, 2
Procter & Gamble, 64–67, 104
  market research by, 141, 146
Pucci, Emilio, 64

Quant, Mary, 117
Quinlan, Mary Lou, 207, 209

Radcliffe, 72
Raphaelson, Joel, 54, 103, 132
Raphaelson, Marikay Hartigan, 53–54, 115
Rattazzi's, 22, 100–101
Rayon Association, 149
Reader's Digest, 105
Reagan, Ronald, 182
Reiss, Elaine, 82
Resor, Stanley, 33
Rohaytyn, Felix, 175
Rolls-Royce, 140
Roman, Ellen, 117
Roman, Ken, 35, 38, 60, 64, 99, *166,* 170–71, 213
Rosen, Marcella, 63
Rosenthal, Alvin, 200
Rosenthal, Leona Mindy. *See* Helmsley, Leona
Roth, Philip, 40, *74,* 76
Roth, Sandy, 40
Rums of Puerto Rico, 6, 160

St. Regis Hotel, New York, 187–88
Salk, Jonas, 90
Salter, Harry, 58–59
Schafly, Phyllis, 91
The School for Scandal, 133
S. C. Johnson Company, 149–51
Screw magazine, 31–32
sex
  in advertising environments, 27–49
  advertising innuendos to, 157, 164–71
  on commercial shoots, 39–42
  divorces resulting from, 42–44
  gender stereotypes and, 157–60, 210
  homosexuality and, 132–33
  at office parties, 37–39
  promotions resulting from, 29
Sex and the Single Girl (Brown), 164–65

sexism, 4, 133–34
  in account assignments, 6, 8–9, 59, 62–69
  awareness of, 54–57
  child-rearing and, 71–84, 91–92, 205, 210
  in colleges, 72–78
  in fashion/clothing, 113–19
  feminist movement and, 55, 131, 157–60, 210
  housewife perceptions and, 55, 122
  menstruation and, 122
  mentorship and, 206–7
  modern, 203–12
  in promotions/salaries, 16–17, 30, 51–69
  in restaurants/clubs, 24–25, 121–22, 129–30
  sex in workplace and, 29–30, 46–49
  stereotypes in advertisements and, 157–60, 210
sexual harassment, 29, 46–49
Shake 'n Bake, 142, 145, 159
Sheridan, Richard Brinsley, 133
Shrimpton, Jean, 117
Sinatra, Frank, 197
Sinclair, Daisy Nieland, 95–96, 114
The Sisters Rosensweig, 44
The $64,000 Question, 10
Smith College, 53, 73
SmokEnders, 107–8
smoking
  cigarette, 103–8
  marijuana, 109–11
StarKist, 146
Steinem, Gloria, 210
Steuben Glass, 6

Tandy, Jessica, 179
Taster's Choice, 158
Taylor, Elizabeth, 169
technology
  communication-based, 119, 125
  modern, 209, 211
  office, 119–20
  television and, 119–20, 125–26
Ted Bates Agency, 7, 135, 147
Time magazine, 10, 57, 174
Toro, 160
Touffou, Château de, France, 35–37, 171
Trager, Olivia, 63
Tums, 7
TWA, 66
Twenty One, 10–11
21 Club, 116–17, 127–28

United Airlines, 166–67
U.S. Rubber, 55

Van Doren, Charles, 10–11
Vanish, 6, 11, 17, 41
Virginia Slims, 203
Volkswagen, 7, 136, 148

Wallach, Anne Tolstoi, 57, 59, 79, 103, 115
Walters, Barbara, 53
Wasserstein, Bruce, 43

Wasserstein, Wendy, 43–44
Wells, Mary. *See* Lawrence, Mary Wells
Wells Rich Greene, 165
  creative revolution and, 135, 138, 147
  "I Love New York" campaign by, 89, 93–94, 173–83, 193
  Maas's work with, 64–69, 89–91, 93–94, 104, 119, 122, 173–83, 193–94, 198
Westhampton Mallet Club, 36
Weston, Susan, 91–92, 117
Whistle Spray Cleaner, 40–41
Withers, Jane, 145, 161
women, career. *See also* advertising industry; child rearing; sexism
  account bias against, 6, 8–9, 59, 62–69
  alcohol consumption by, 102–3
  child-rearing by, 2–4, 11, 15–16, 23–24, 71–92, 113, 123, 204–12
  competition between, 60–61
  contemporary state of, 203–12
  day in the life of, 1–25
  dietary habits and, 123–25, 126–30
  dress/attire of, 113–18
  mentorship between, 206–7
  salaries of, 51–69
  sex in workplace and, 27–49
Women in Communications, 185
working mothers. *See* child rearing; women, career
Wrangel, George, 101, 140
Wright, Frank Lloyd, 151

Young & Rubicam, 53
  alcohol consumption at, 95
  diversity at, 132
  Mad Men's association to, 27
  pregnancy policy at, 80
  sexual trysts at, 27–28, 30

Zarem, Bobby, 174